HG
939.5
.R62

Robbins, Lionel Charles
Robbins, Baron 1898 –

Against inflation :
speeches in the 2nd
chamber 1965 – 1977

DISCARDED

	DATE DUE		

AGAINST INFLATION

AGAINST INFLATION

Speeches in the Second Chamber
1965–1977

Lord Robbins

HM HOLMES & MEIER PUBLISHERS, INC.
IMPORT DIVISION
30 Irving Place, New York, N.Y. 10003

First published 1979 by
THE MACMILLAN PRESS LTD
London and Basingstoke
Associated companies in Delhi
Dublin Hong Kong Johannesburg Lagos
Melbourne New York Singapore Tokyo

Printed in Great Britain by
REDWOOD BURN LTD
Trowbridge and Esher

British Library Cataloguing in Publication Data

Robbins, Lionel, *Baron Robbins*
    Against inflation
    1. Inflation (Finance) – Great Britain –
    Addresses, essays, lectures
    I. Title
    332.4'1   HG939.5

    ISBN 0-333-25974-2

To my friends in different parts of the House

Contents

Preface

As its title implies, the centre of gravity of the following collection is the decline in the value of money, which, in greater degree than in most other Western financial centres, has affected the economy of this country for more than a quarter of a century. During this period diagnosis of this movement and its effects, internal and external, have been a more or less continuous preoccupation of economists concerned with the practical uses of their subject. I myself have written on these subjects on many occasions. But in my position as a cross-bencher in the Second Chamber at Westminster I have had special opportunities for observing the evolution of events and policies as they emerged; and it has occurred to me that the reactions involved, as reflected in successive interventions in debate on my part, may have some interest supplementary to more systematic treatment elsewhere.*

Accordingly I have here collected such of my speeches as have relevance in this connection. Save for the correction of obvious mistakes in reproduction, the omission of unnecessary references to other speeches or interruptions and certain unessential digressions or perorations, they are reproduced as delivered and in chronological order. Needless to say, as I have re-read them, I can see points which should have been better emphasised and objections which I could wish to have anticipated. But I have made no attempt at revision other than the instances mentioned above, preferring that they should be read as they were conceived, either in preparation or delivery, as contributions to debates rather than as systematic disquisitions standing on their own.

It is inevitable that this form of presentation involves some repetition and considerable variation of emphasis. The repetition I do not regret, in view of comments sometimes ventilated by friends abroad not in close touch with the *minutiae* of our local controversies. I am glad rather than otherwise that the main points of view which have inspired my outlook over these years, should be demonstrated to have been reiterated so often. But the variation of emphasis, deriving at least partly from variation of

* A more or less systematic outline of my fundamental beliefs in this respect is contained in the papers reprinted in my *Money, Trade and International Relations* (1971). See also my *Memorandum of Evidence* to the *Radcliffe Committee on the Working of the Monetary System* (Memoranda of Evidence, Vol. 3, pp. 211–19) and my critique of the *Report* of that Committee in the collection mentioned above—a paper to which I attach especial importance.

aspects under discussion, perhaps deserves some further elucidation. I
would like therefore in this Preface to state briefly and baldly the chief
principles which have guided my approach.

1. Inflation in the sense of a fall in the purchasing power of money is
an evil—at least if it exceeds a very small percentage rate. It is an economic
evil as regards the smooth running of the economic system in that it falsifies
expectations, distorts the allocation of productive services intended by
consumers and investors, encourages undesirable speculation and, unless
other areas are inflating at the same rate in relation to productivity, creates
imbalance in external financial relations. It is an ethical evil in that it
imposes unfair burdens on those members of the country who are unable to
secure adjustments of their money incomes in compensation; and it
involves governments in fraudulent representations of the real implications
of the money returns on public borrowing. It is a social evil in that the
prospects of quick gains foster corruption and social divisiveness.

2. The initiatory causes of inflation are various: demand inflation
arising from excessive public expenditure; cost inflation arising from
demands for rates of pay disproportionate to productivity at constant
prices or adverse changes in the terms of international trade. But in neither
case is inflation likely to go far, if there is adequate control of aggregate
national expenditure in relation to the value of the national product
estimated at constant prices. This is the invincible platitude from which all
considerations of policy must begin.

3. Such policy necessarily involves direct control of the supply of
money and credit. But it does not exclude indirect control by fiscal
measures. On general grounds I believe that the main policies of public
taxation and expenditure should be based on considerations other than
those relating to macro-economic equilibrium. I am also opposed to 'fine
tuning' in this latter connection, for obvious reasons relating to the
statistical margins of error involved in such operations. But, especially in
times of acute instability in the value of money, I think it is unwise to pass a
self-denying ordinance in respect of any fiscal measures devoted to curing
such troubles. Here I part company with extreme monetarists.

4. The curbing of inflation should not be described as *de*flation. It is
easy to fall into this habit in informal talk; and candour compels me to
admit that I myself did so in the first few speeches printed in this collection.
But it is wrong and misleading: it fails to distinguish a rate of increase and
movements in that rate. Deflation is a positive deficiency of aggregate
expenditure in relation to output at constant prices; and, as we saw in the
thirties, can be also a very great evil. But reducing the rate of inflation is *not*
deflation. Inflation may still proceed at a dangerous level when the rate has

been considerably reduced. This is the state of affairs here—as this preface is being drafted.

5. If, when inflation is in full swing, the excess of aggregate expenditure over the value of production at constant prices is suddenly reduced to zero or near zero, the result is likely to be a disastrous depression. The sensible policy is a gradual—though not too gradual— reduction of the rate. Of course this will be more quickly effective the greater the rise in aggregate production—if such a rise takes place. But, if the excess of aggregate expenditure is anything but very small, it is pure folly to rely only on this latter possibility.

6. In branches of economic activity where the government is the main employer, it is essential that it should have a permanent incomes policy taking into account the principle laid down above in paragraph 2; otherwise the facilities which it has for creating additional money will tend inevitably to inflation.

7. If, during a period when the excess of aggregate expenditure is being brought under control and reduced, there can be engineered restraint in price and pay claims on the part of monopolistic associations, this will have the double effect (a) of mitigating the upward movement of prices, and (b) of reducing the tendency to increasing unemployment. This is the rationale of such restraint. It is to be noted, however, that restraints of pay imposed from the centre, unless managed much more skilfully than hitherto, have themselves a tendency to breed division between the various groups affected and thus to lead to eventual failure.

8. The tendency in the Free World at large during the last few years for a breakdown in orderly relationships between the currencies of the various states concerned clearly arises from different rates of inflation in the different financial centres. In such circumstances floating rates may become inevitable. But they themselves may create new difficulties which only very large and powerful financial areas will not find highly embarrassing, especially as regards capital transactions.

In surveying what I have said during the years which these speeches cover, I am conscious of all sorts of shortcomings as regards exposition and emphasis. But I have little to retract. I am certainly not ashamed of having supported the policy of not devaluing after 1964 when the Labour Government inherited the considerable difficulties caused by the so-called 'dash for freedom' of its Conservative predecessor. It seemed to me then, and it seems to me now that these difficulties, if firmly dealt with, were not such as to justify the breach of good faith which devaluation would involve with creditors who had lent us money on our assurance that a stable rate of exchange would be maintained; and I did not change my mind in this respect until the results of the seamen's strike of 1966 had made this course of action unavoidable. I do regret, however, not emphasising even more than I did the necessity for this policy to be backed by sterner internal action. This was never foreign to my thought at this time. But in some occasional expression of hopes that the measures which were being taken might be successful, I allowed myself to be too impressed by sympathy for what was being done by the Government against continual criticism from back-benchers with no sense of economic realities, not to voice sufficiently strongly fears that it might not be enough.

For the rest of the period covered I am content to let the record speak for itself.

At the point at which the collection ends, a stage had been reached at which the rate of inflation was being reduced, a surplus on current account of the balance of payments was emerging and speculative money, instead of moving out of the City, was coming in. In the debate in which this situation was discussed, I made a speech in which, while readily acknowledging these favourable symptoms, I warned of continuing dangers and new problems. At the conclusion of my remarks, I was challenged by Lady Birk to say whether I was optimistic or pessimistic. To this I gave a non-committal reply. In this I was perfectly candid. I find it more difficult to peer into the future of our economic development now than perhaps ever before in my lifetime. But of this I am sure: that, if the lessons of the truly deplorable history with which these speeches have been concerned have been well and truly learned, to that extent we shall be better off than we should have been otherwise. If they have not, if the old futile belief reasserts itself that we can pursue growth and employment at the expense of the value of money, then our future will be dark indeed.

ROBBINS

The London School of Economics
January 1978

1 Internal Inflation and the Future Rate of Exchange

Finance (No. 2) Bill Second Reading and Remaining Stages; 4 August 1965

My Lords, in addressing myself to the subject matter of this debate, I confess that I have never felt more grateful for the asylum presented by the cross-benches. We are confronted with a crisis in our affairs which is more menacing than any since the war, and as I myself conceive the issues it is difficult to adopt an attitude agreeable in all respects to either side of the House. The situation is indeed grim, grimmer, I think, than has appeared from any of the speeches made this afternoon so far.

Internally we are confronted with brisk inflation. Despite Mr Brown's devoted efforts, the incomes policy is not working. Prices, as measured by the Cost of Living Index, have been rising at a rate of more than $6\frac{1}{2}$ per cent per annum, which means that all those who live on fixed incomes are likely to be that degree worse off. And if one takes account of the shrinkage in the real value of their holdings, those who hold government stock yielding $6\frac{1}{2}$ per cent—an almost unprecedented rate in our financial history—will be lending at a zero rate of interest, and those who do not get $6\frac{1}{2}$ per cent will be lending at negative rates.

Externally the position is still worse. Our first line cash reserves have shrunk to a sum which would hardly purchase a week's imports. If we were not propped up by loans from abroad, the present parity of the pound would have disintegrated long ago. And although with the support we are receiving and the extraordinary reserves which we can muster we have managed to survive thus far, the future is very uncertain. The fundamental malaise of our balance of payments persists. It is true that the deficit is substantially smaller than it was a year ago, but it is still running at an alarmingly high rate and there are no prospects of a very rapid improvement.

Why has this happened? I think we get our perspective all wrong in this connection if we try to put the blame on deficiencies of productivity. I do not wish to deny the importance of such deficiencies. No one who has had the misfortune to have to use either London Airport or British Railways could be blind to shortcomings in that respect; and it would not be difficult to find a similar state of affairs in parts of the private sector. Nor should I wish to deny that, if productivity had increased faster and incomes had not increased, the situation would be substantially better. But these are long run considerations, highly important as regards our eventual rate of growth, but largely beside the point in relation to present difficulties. You do not get such sudden increases in aggregate production. That is why mere exhortations to produce more, to the neglect of other essential measures, are so pathetically irrelevant. You do not get a sudden emergence of difficulties in the balance of payments because growth is not as rapid as it might be.

But such a change, such a rapid emergence of difficulties, is the essence of the situation with which we are confronted. Three years ago we were not doing badly. Our exports were reasonably competitive, our imports not excessive. The figures for 1962 showed a surplus. Then last year we were out of balance to the tune of some £750 million; and even now, after all that has been done, that formidable deficit has been reduced by only half, if that. Is it really plausible to assume that such spectacular variations are the reflection of changes in productivity? I doubt it.

But if we reject explanation in terms of productivity, where are we to look? The obvious answer, I suggest, is in terms of expenditure. If aggregate expenditure grows faster than production, then the inevitable consequences are rising prices, lengthening delivery dates, increasing imports and increasing obstacles to a commensurate increase in exports. Surely this is what has happened. I should not wish to deny the influence of other adverse factors. But if we try to get things in broad proportion, I see no escape from the conclusion that the main cause of our present difficulties has been excessive aggregate expenditure. Given the fundamental disposition to save and spend, and the probable rate of increase in production, our fiscal and monetary arrangements have been such as to produce a situation in which domestic inflation and external disequilibrium were more or less inevitable. After all, this is not the first time that this sort of thing has happened. This is where we came in before.

In such circumstances, I must say that I see little point in much of the current recrimination about responsibility. I do not see how members of the late Government can repudiate some blame for failure to prevent the emergence of excess expenditure. They were in control, and they did not apply the measures of restraint that were necessary. But what ever they have done since coming into office—I shall be speaking of that later—I do not think that members of the present Government have much justification for reproaching their predecessors. I do not remember much talk on their part in the past of the necessity for going slow and curbing the rate of expansion. Indeed, I think the former Chancellor would be entitled to say to his critics, 'True, I made a mistake. I underestimated the expansive forces. But if I had taken the advice I was given I should have underestimated them even more.'

The fact is, surely, that public opinion has been in something of a muddle on this subject. We are all still suffering from the traumatic effect of the Great Depression of the thirties—the waste of manpower, the loss of production; and, regardless of the fact that the conspicuous phenomenon of the last quarter of a century has been inflation rather than deflation, we tend to exaggerate the danger of the latter and ignore the danger of the former. We are so afraid of running the economic machine at under-capacity that we are always tending to run it beyond its capacity to work without rising prices and difficulties in the balance of payments. We are so barren of invention that we seem to think that the only cure for some long lasting unemployment in the North East and parts of Scotland is to blow up the rest of the system until developing industries elsewhere find it almost impossible to recruit labour. And then, when repeated difficulties of this kind make it impossible altogether to ignore the dangers, we tend to deceive ourselves with the belief that if only the employers and the trade unions would be reasonable, all would be well.

I am not one of those who oppose any incomes policy. I am quite sure that in an economy such as ours something of the sort is desirable, if only to regularise matters in the public sector. But I am sure that all experience shows that employers and trade unionists alike would have to be recruited from some other planet before, in the face of pressures of the kind to which they have been exposed since the war, they abstained from attempting to raise wages and prices. I admire greatly the spirit which underlies Mr George Brown's endeavours; but I am sure he will not succeed unless the pressure of demand is abated. And I would say, as regards public opinion, that the most urgent need is the realisation that, as has been recently argued by the OECD Report, to which allusion has already been made, it is 'Go-Stop', rather than 'Stop-Go', policies which underlie most of our recurring difficulties.

In such circumstances, I find it wrong to withhold tribute to members of the Government for the broad conceptions with which they are tackling our present difficulties. I say 'broad conceptions', for I can think of points which are not mere details on which I have many doubts and reservations. I regret the timing of the deflationary measures. A stiffer dose last autumn might have avoided the necessity for still stiffer doses now. I wonder whether what has yet been done is sufficient to prevent grave continuing difficulties. And I regret very much indeed that so much of the pressure is put on the investment rather than the consumption end: that it bears on provision for the future—roads, public utilities, universities—rather than on enjoyment in the present. In my judgment, a stronger dose of the regulator at an early stage would have been preferable to much that has been done recently to discourage new construction. But, when all that has been said, I think we should admire the empiricism with which the Government has tackled the difficulties, putting the strength of the economy before adherence to inappropriate dogma and ideology. And I should regard with considerable distaste any attempt on the part of opposing parties to make capital out of the ardours and endurances which such a policy may entail. I wish I could give similar praise to some of the more permanent measures embodied in the Bill which is the pretext for to-day's discussion. But, where these are concerned, I find myself in sharp opposition, both as regards substance and as regards the mode of their introduction.

Let me restrict myself, however, to more immediate problems? It is one of the drawbacks of the particular measures which have been adopted that they must take some time to show their effects. At present, despite all that has been done to deflate the economy, we are still in a state of high boom. So far, the curbs on investment are operating only in the planning back-rooms and in forward contracts. That is one reason why I should so much have preferred the use of the regulator, which can be relied on to operate strongly within a short period. But it is difficult to believe that they will not eventually produce some effect. I personally should be surprised if there is not some braking visible by mid-winter.

The momentous question remains, how much? Will the measures which have been adopted so far be sufficient to check the inflation and restore health to the external balance? Remember always as regards this latter, that we have not only to wipe out the present deficit, but also to repay what we have borrowed and to create sufficient surplus to play a suitable part in the development and pacification of the world as a whole. To the question, 'Are the measures sufficient?', I find it difficult to give a definite answer, for there are so many unknowns involved. I would only say that if the Government—who should have better information than the rest of us—have any reason to doubt the effectiveness of what has been done up to date, they should not hesitate to act further. And they should not be deterred by the fear of depression later on. I find it difficult to believe that the present degree of deflation, or even some intensification thereof, is likely to cause severe depression.

After all, we are still operating at a capacity of 98·8 per cent as measured by the employment percentage. Contraction to the figure which, in the past, has meant something like equilibrium could not by the wildest use of language be called a disaster. And if by any chance it seemed that the mark was being overshot there are plenty of means available to reverse the process. Too often, since the war, the adoption of policies to curb undue expansion has been delayed on the pretext that depression was just round the corner—as if you should delay operating the fire hose for fear of rainy weather the next winter. Our business is to solve the problem which now confronts us, not to shirk it because other problems may arise later on.

Amid all these uncertainties it is natural that there should be prevalent in many quarters queries concerning the future rate of exchange; and although, doubtless, there are considerations of prudence which should guide what one says in this connection, I do not think that it should not be mentioned in this House. When every economist and every businessman with foreign connections is discussing this question, it does not seem very grown up to proceed as if it did not exist. Let me say at once that I approve of the decision which the Government took last year to maintain the rate of exchange. In my judgment, it would have been an ignominious thing to have resorted to devaluation without making any effort to see whether the situation could be cured without it. It would also have been a dishonourable thing with so much foreign money here, which had been so placed in the belief that the rate would be maintained and would not be abandoned without a struggle.

However, I should also like to say that I am not one of those who would be opposed to devaluation in any circumstances. As the only surviving U.K. economist delegate to the Bretton Woods conference, I still believe firmly that, if an economy finds itself in what the statutes of the International Monetary Fund describe as a 'fundamental disequilibrium', then, rather than inflict on itself catastrophic deflation in order to maintain existing rates, it is better for it to cut its losses and, with due consultation with other centres, adjust to a new parity. But, my Lords, the governing word is 'fundamental'. The men who drafted that statute, I can assure your Lordships, had in mind the disequilibria of the inter-war period, the great depression, when severe contractions and mass unemployment were insufficient to restore the position of countries such as Great Britain and the gold bloc. They were not thinking of the disequilibria of economies running at 98·8 per cent of capacity. They were not creating an instrument providing for changes of parity on each and every occasion when spending gets out of line with domestic production and the international conditions of supply and demand. And when I think of the perilous dislocations in the world at large that would inevitably be caused by the devaluation of sterling at this juncture, I cannot but applaud the decision of Her Majesty's Government to try to fight it out the hard way.

But supposing that, as time goes on, all reasonable measures fail to work. Supposing that the withdrawal of capital becomes insupportable, or that it becomes clear that the external balance will not be restored at the existing sterling rate, save by measures which would recreate the unemployment conditions of the interwar era, then I have little doubt that we should choose the alternative of devaluation—or rather, as I should prefer, letting the rate float until the time had come when we could see what permanent rate was appropriate.

Then, supposing that day should come—I profoundly hope it will not—let no one think that that solution would be an easy way out of our troubles. Let no one think that just letting the sterling rate go would mean an end to the need for restraint and circumspection; and that, if the pound were devalued, we could just heave a sigh of relief and begin the next spending spree. We have seen that sort of thing elsewhere; and both theory and experience combine to teach us that if, in the event of devaluation, a strong curb is not still kept on aggregate expenditure, the whole process begins again—indeed, the depreciation of the rate of exchange itself becomes a factor in a further inflationary process. I pray that we shall not have to contemplate this danger. But if we do, then it is quite fundamental that we should see to it that the adjustment of the rate of exchange is an adjustment to an internally stable position.

2 A Breathing Space and Premature Optimism

Motion: The Economic Situation; 9 February 1966

My Lords, when we last discussed this subject, on the occasion of the Finance Bill in the summer, the position was very grim indeed. Funds were pouring out of the country at a disturbing rate. Rates of exchange were sustained only by the lavish use of support from abroad. The Press and the clubs were reverberating with hints or fears of imminent devaluation.

To-day things look decidedly better. The pressure has eased. Rates of exchanges are at a level which suggests that money is still coming back to London. The reserves have been increasing for some months. But, gratifying though it is to have moved out of this region of extreme danger, I find it difficult to share the euphoria prevalent in many quarters about our present prospects. Indeed, I marvel at the volatility of public opinion about a situation which, apart from these squalls and tempests on the capital account, still presents the same basic problems as it did last summer.

First, we are still in a position of serious weakness as regards liquid debt. I do not know the exact position as regards emergency credits, but it is clear that we still have to repay what we have borrowed from the International Monetary Fund. And even if this were done, even if our reserves stood at the pre-crisis level without borrowing, it would surely be abundantly clear that they were not high enough then. Current discussion seems to hold that this can all be looked after by improved arrangements regarding international liquidity. But this is far too complacent; such arrangements are not yet in being. Even if they were, they would not excuse us from the necessity of some strengthening of our own position which, having regard to our external obligations, has long tended to be dangerously weak. And let no one evade the responsibility by arguing as if such a policy were out of the question. One has only to look elsewhere, at Germany and France, for instance, to see what is possible without undue sacrifice.

But, secondly, quite apart from the capital position, it is evident that the position on current account is still far from satisfactory. It is true that we are not running the unprecedented deficit of 1964 and that the recent trade returns have been more favourable. But it is equally true that we are not yet in balance. The figures given by the noble Lord, Lord Shepherd, show a position which is certainly not conducive to any equanimity. If it does not get better, we cannot go on. For the time being the crisis of confidence has been stilled and our credit is restored. We have achieved a breathing space. But confidence in the capital position depends upon health in the current account. If we cannot achieve equilibrium on the current account within a measurable time, the crisis will recur—I would say with increased violence. If we cannot achieve a surplus, then we cannot repay our debts, we cannot strengthen the reserve, and we cannot play our part in the political stabilisation and economic development of the world.

What then, my Lords, are the prospects? I am not ashamed to say that I am not prepared to make exact predictions. There are projections available—and some have been indirectly alluded to this afternoon—some hopeful, some not so hopeful. Doubtless these have some use as indicating the complicated arithmetical implications of certain quantitative assumptions. It would be foolish to say that this sort of thing should not be done, but it would be equally foolish to say that it has the status of a genuine forecast—a projection is not a prediction. The actual progress of events is the resultant of many factors, so many of which are not within our control, that we deceive ourselves and entertain false notions of policy if we assume that quantitative prediction in this field is at all within our grasp.

Much less ambitious but, in my judgment, much more fruitful, is to ask whether the underlying conditions are or are not propitious to further improvement. We know that the state of the balance of payments depends, if not wholly at any rate in large part, upon the relationship of incomes and prices here to incomes and prices elsewhere. We know that if our balance is in deficit, then if this is to be cured—still more if a surplus is to be achieved—it is certainly desirable that prices and incomes here should rise less rapidly than elsewhere. Obviously that is not the whole of the story: there are changes in productivity and in the conditions of demand to be taken into account, and also the influence of changes in tariffs and quantitative controls. But as a first approximation the principle I have enunciated will do. It would really be a most astonishing fluke if, with prices and incomes here increasing faster than elsewhere, the balance of payments became more favourable.

Now if we approach our problem this way, it is pretty clear that the present position is by no means free from danger. I am not prepared to diagnose the trends in the leading areas elsewhere—though I should be surprised if at present there were strong inflationary tendencies operating in more than a minority of cases. But we know that at a time when it is imperative that our own income levels should not rise more rapidly than productivity, in fact the reverse has been the case. In the twelve months up to last October, average earnings rose by something of the order of magnitude of 8 per cent Does anyone in his senses believe that productivity rose in like proportion, however it is measured? Whatever projections based upon the assumption of no inflation may suggest, a movement of this sort in the economic level must render them largely irrelevant. Indeed, if it continues—and I hope it will not—I am clear not only that the balance of payments will continue adverse, but also that it will prove eventually impossible to maintain the present parity of sterling. I am not saying that this will happen—far from it. I am saying only that it will happen if we cannot curb the inflation.

To guard against these dangers, the fashionable remedy has been an incomes policy. Our little world of *soi-disant* experts arouse in people a feeling of contempt for the policies of financial prudence and the allegedly baneful influences of the Treasury and the Bank of England which, they seem to think, are the chief obstacles to limitless prosperity. If you remonstrate with them gently, and remind them that hitherto in world history beyond a certain point high-pressure spending has always led to inflation and trouble with balances of payments, the reply is always, 'Oh, well, we need an incomes policy.'

My Lords, I submit that what we need most of all is more objectivity and less wishful thinking about this subject. Let me make myself clear. Few sensible people, I suppose, are against an incomes policy in the public sector. Where there is no compulsion from calculations of profit and loss, there, if there is no clear policy concerning the extent to which incomes can be allowed to advance, things will get hopelessly out of gear, not only within the public sector but throughout the economy as a whole. I will not pause to ask what that policy should be: it is quite a complicated problem. I only insist that so far as the public sector is concerned—and it is a big sector—an incomes policy is of paramount necessity.

Nor, my Lords, do I wish to blow cold upon the idea of restraint and good sense in collective bargaining wherever it takes place. Unlike some noble Lords, I have watched with sympathy and admiration the efforts of Mr George Brown and other men of good will to spread a greater sense of responsibility in matters of this sort. I agree that if we could count on a universal disposition among employers not to concede wage claims which would compel rises in prices, and among trade unionists not to make them, then we could rely on a fair prospect for the purchasing power of money and stability in foreign exchanges.

But can we depend on this? I sincerely wish I could say yes, but neither general reasoning nor past experience affords much warrant for such optimism. General reasoning suggests that when the economy is working to such capacity that the number of jobs being offered is greater than the number of applications for them, in other words a labour shortage, there is a tendency for employers to bid against one another and for the trade unions to increase their claims. Analysis of past experience shows this working out with depressing regularity.

Professor Phillips, a colleague of mine at the London School of Economics, has worked on this problem with results which have a significant moral for policy. Professor Phillips finds that over a long period of time, with very few exceptions, when the use of capacity, as measured in terms of employment, has passed a percentage of somewhere between 97·5 and 98, there has been a tendency for incomes to rise faster than productivity and thus to produce rising prices and difficulties with the balance of payments. I have no doubt that many of our troubles since the war are to be explained in this way. We have been pushing too hard and have often fallen over in consequence.

At the present time we are well beyond what may be called the 'Phillips point', and I find it difficult to believe that the present movement of incomes is not still further evidence of the tendencies which these investigations have unearthed. It is not to deny the necessity of a coherent policy for the Government as employer, or to deprecate appeals for moderation and good sense throughout the labour market as a whole, to believe that if the economy is over-loaded then we shall not save ourselves for inflation by talking of an incomes policy. There can be a successful incomes policy only if the pressure on capacity is not too great.

Fortunately for all of us, the present Government, while trying manfully to bring an incomes policy into operation, have not been prepared to rely on these attempts alone. They have resorted to further measures, in both the fiscal and the monetary spheres, intended to take the heat out of the system; and it is doubtless to the adoption of these measures that we owe the restoration of confidence abroad. The foreigner will believe in the effectiveness of incomes policy when he sees a movement of earnings more in line with productivity. But, rightly or wrongly, he pays immediate attention to measures operating on aggregate expenditure. I think great credit is due to the present Government for having confronted our difficulties in a pragmatic spirit and for having had the courage to impose curbs and restraints which in the nature of things were likely to prove unpopular.

The great question at the moment is: will these measures bite? Will the present restraints on expenditure be sufficient to arrest the inflation and restore the balance of payments? I confess I am still very apprehensive. The inflationary forces are still strong and I doubt whether we have yet done enough to bring them under control.

In any case, two considerations seem to me to be important. The first is that if present measures are insufficient we should nerve ourselves to take more. When so much has been done already it would be an ignominious and damaging thing to abandon the struggle and let the pound go and the value of money depreciate with a use of capacity which is still some 98·8 per cent of the labour force. I suggest that this is no time to talk of easements in the forthcoming Budget. The serious question is whether a 'no change' Budget will be enough.

The second consideration is that if and when this policy begins to act at all strongly, whatever government are in power will find themselves exposed to a new danger—the temptation to relax before the restraints have become fully effective. And there will be a temptation, too, to whatever party is in opposition—a temptation to claim that, if it were in power, these ardours and endurances would not be necessary. My Lords, I hope very much these temptations will be resisted. If they are not then certainly our troubles will begin over again. It is the distinction of the present Government not to have flinched from stern measures, and I submit that it is the duty of all of us, whether or not we agree with the Government in other ways, to give these measures continuing support.

3 Fear of Depression in a Period of Overheating

Motion: The Economic Situation; 28 July 1966

My Lords, reverting to the immediate crisis which overhangs this discussion, the first thing I should like to say is that we are clearly not yet out of the wood. I hope and trust that the measures announced last week will convince holders of sterling that at last we are in earnest and that this will quell the psychological tornado which broke out some three weeks ago. But we deceive ourselves if we suppose that all that has happened is just another piece of bad luck—the seamen's strike, the world rise in interest rates, M. Pompidou's observations on British economic policy, and so on and so forth. The fact is—let us face it—that we are still in an acute position of long-term financial disequilibrium. We are not within sight of financing our overseas purchases and expenditure without running further into debt. For many months it has been becoming clearer that the prospect of balancing the account by the end of this year was illusory and that unless there was an unexpected improvement, the knowledge that this was so was bound to lead to another crisis.

I am not speaking now with hindsight. The present position was predictable. The last time we had a debate on this subject I allowed myself to say that if the inflation continued, not only would the balance continue adverse, but it would prove eventually impossible to maintain the present parity of sterling. I added:

> The inflationary forces are still strong and I doubt whether we have yet done enough to bring them under control [*Official Report*, Vol. 272, col. 790; 9/2/66].

The ultimate test, therefore, of last week's measures is not merely that they damp down the recent speculative movement but, further, that they arrest the inflation and create a situation in which the state of the balance of payments once more permits us to pay our way.

Turning to the measures themselves, I can see a good deal in detail which I could have wished otherwise. I personally greatly regret the cuts in investment and wish that more of what had to be cut had been imposed on consumption. We shall all be worse off if the development of the infrastructure of nationalised industry is held up and the process of industrial development is unduly interrupted. I share the fears of the noble Lord, Lord Kahn, in that respect. I cannot believe that consumption in general could not have sustained much more than the comparatively small increases involved by the 10 per cent regulator. I could wish, too, that there had been some cuts in subsidies where no severe hardship would be involved. I shall never believe that, old-age pensioners and chronic invalids apart, the rest of us cannot afford the price of ten cigarettes when we go to collect our prescriptions.

But we are at a moment of grave national crisis, and surely it would be wrong to let objections to particular measures inhibit unequivocal support for he general policy of restricting expenditure. If I were an outside commentator, speaking to the world at large, I would express the view that last week's announcement marked a watershed in policy in this country. It marked recognition—genuine recognition at last—that you cannot run an economy of this sort, so dependent on its external connections, on the basis of creeping inflation and excess use of capacity. It marked an end of the belief that a situation of this sort can be dealt with by soft measures and loud exhortations. Although quantitative prediction in these matters is a fool's game, since we live from day to day and have to adjust our appraisals accordingly, I would venture to express the hope that the amount which it is now proposed to take out of the stream of spending should be sufficient to accomplish its purpose and produce a more solid foundation for growth and prosperity; and, whatever my reservations on the appropriateness of certain cuts, I should wish to defend that policy against its critics— to defend, that is to say, the general policy of disinflation at this time.

The first criticism that I should like to controvert is the criticism that instead of deflating we should have devalued. I welcome greatly the declaration by the noble Lord, Lord Shepherd, in this connection, expressing the firm decision of the Government not to resort to this expedient. I do not think indeed that in present circumstances this view that we should have devalued has much practical applicability. On the most cynical outlook, there is a limit to the number of undertakings recently given that one can go back on, just like that. But I know this view is held, let us face it, by some of the ablest and sincerest among us, and I think it deserves a considered answer. I do not think that the answer is only that devaluation without deflation would be dangerous. That is true indeed. But against that argument it is still open to the devaluationist to reply that, with his solution, the deflation need be less.

In my judgment, therefore, the true answer is an appeal to common honesty. I do not think that devaluation can be ruled out in all circumstances. The Bretton Woods Agreement specifically made provision for such adjustments in certain conditions. If there was mass unemployment on an extensive scale and no prospect of improvement without

further deflation, if we were obviously in what the statutes of the
International Monetary Fund call 'a position of fundamental disequilibrium', then clearly these conditions would be satisfied. But I do suggest that
it would be a plain breach of duty, both to our partners in the International
Monetary Agreement and to our creditors—to those who have put their
money here, trusting that we should keep our word—if we were to devalue
now, when the level of unemployment is almost at an all-time record low
for peace time and the economy is still in a state of inflationary boom. I
have suggested already that it would be wildly inexpedient, having regard
to the obligations which have already been entered into in the last weeks
and months. But I hope I have shown that there are deeper reasons of good
faith and common decency why at this time we should not contemplate
such a policy.

The next criticism I would consider is that which arises from fear of
unemployment. This is a fear which inspires the attitude of all sorts of
serious minded people, and it is clearly one which deserves the most
respectful consideration. I personally always speak on this subject with
considerable trepidation and diffidence. In the inter-war period when
mass unemployment actually prevailed, I was on the wrong side: I opposed
measures of reflation which I now think might have eased the situation;
and, although I do not flatter myself that my attitude influenced action in
any respect, I shall always most seriously regret having done so. But, my
Lords, we are not confronted with a situation of mass unemployment. We
are confronted with a position in which, in many parts of the country, the
number of vacancies available vastly surpasses the number of applicants
coming forward. We are far past the point at which experience shows that
price inflation and balance-of-payments difficulties almost invariably set
in. In 1939 the late Lord Keynes, whose record in this respect, in sharp
contrast to mine, was utterly above suspicion, warned us that if there were
550,000 unemployed, we should be confronted with the problems of full
employment in an acute form. My reference is to a turnover article in *The
Times* in that year. And remember that half a million then was a
considerably larger fraction of the working force than half a million would
be now.

The fact is, in my judgment, that the use of capacity to-day as measured
in terms of labour is so excessive that while it persists, unless we are willing
to resort to complete regimentation and direction of the labour force, there
can be little hope of redeployment of labour sufficient to meet the incessant
incidence of change. It is impossible to achieve mobility with an army,
almost every able-bodied member of which is already committed to action.
So the necessity of adaptation to changing circumstances must involve, for
those who are changing jobs, a brief period in which in the statistical sense
they are not employed; and experience seems to show that this degree of
adaptability is not to be secured with a use of the labour force much over
97·7 per cent or 97·8 per cent.

Now if such a slackening of employment were only to be secured by the permanent or long-lasting unemployment of the persons thus enumerated, I would say it was indeed a position of extreme gravity. But this is not at all likely. The composition of the statistical percentage is in fact a continually changing one, over a substantial part of the field; and what is to be expected from a more moderate use of capacity is, in substantial measure, merely a lengthening for a few days or weeks of the time of transfer to a new job. If there be areas where this does not happen, if there be areas where there is a danger of human capital rotting month after month in enforced idleness, I would unhesitatingly say that that was an occasion for preventive action. But I should not think that such action would appropriately take the form of blowing up the rest of the economy or keeping it blown up in a state of inflation and international unbalance.

A closely related criticism is that which emphasises the dangers of a chain reaction of adverse movements. The fear is often expressed that as a result of the disinflationary measures recently announced the economy may be pushed into a nose dive and that before we know where we are we shall be in a position of industrial inactivity and waste. It is sometimes said that already the signs are ominous of a falling-off of activity and that in such circumstances disinflationary measures will only make things worse.

As I said earlier, I see grounds for some fear in this connection. I do not like that part of the package which acts on long-term investment. Investment which is damped down necessarily takes time to get started again, and in the interval there may be further adverse repercussions. I wish the contradiction had been more concentrated at the consumption end. But I cannot share the view that the application of the brake need necessarily involve an intolerable slowing down. I am clear that if such a danger were to show itself, there are many ways in which it could be arrested. In the inter-war period, when we used to discuss theoretically control of the trade cycle, it used to be said that the chief problem was to discover ways of initiating recovery rather than curbing the boom.

In the post-war event I think experience has proved otherwise. We now know what some of us did not realise then, that when there is real slack in the system recourse to certain fiscal measures can soon set things right without danger; the regulator can begin to act, so to speak, overnight. But we have not discovered painless methods of controlling inflation. I therefore hope very much that the Government will not be inhibited in carrying out their manifest duty now by fears of what may happen later on. Surely it is the dismal record of our history since the war that, again and again, when quite a slight touch on the brakes would have kept the economy stable, fears of this sort have been the enemy of action. And now, when the house is blazing, surely it would be folly to desist from using the hose for fear that later on there may be floods, which can be dealt with in other ways.

Finally, there comes fears of the effects of these measures on our long-term productivity. Here I think the position is more complicated. I certainly do not think that a reduction of the inflationary heat in the economy will be damaging to productivity per head—that is very unlikely. I do not think it need be damaging to future rates of growth; to go forward cautiously is to avoid upsetting reverses. But, as I have said, I do regret the curbs on investment. I think there is real danger here which needs watching. And let me add that I certainly think there is still much in our general economic policies which works against the improvement of productivity.

It is clear to me, for instance—to say perhaps the most unpopular thing I could say—that the present policy in regard to rents is a definite impediment to mobility; you cannot hold rents below the equilibrium point without positively creating housing shortages; and I am bound to say that, in my judgment, the selective employment tax will put a premium on labour hoarding when labour hoarding should in fact be discouraged. I completely agree with the noble Viscount, Lord Chandos, in this connection. And although all hope of resolving a crisis of this magnitude by increases of productivity alone seems to me to be grotesquely inappropriate to the immediate needs of the situation, I very much hope that the Government will review all their policies with this criterion in mind. In the long run all our positive hopes of growth depend upon this factor, and we should not let any dogmas or shibboleths stand in the way of achieving it.

4 Devaluation and the Dangers Ahead

Motion: Devaluation of the Pound Sterling; 21 November 1967

My Lords, first, I should like to align myself very strongly with those who hold that this is no occasion for rejoicing. We can surely all agree that we have suffered a great setback. We have incurred a deep humiliation. It may be that one has some sense of relief that the claims of one's creditors are reduced to 17s. 2d. in the pound, but a man must be very insensitive morally who does not feel ashamed that their confidence has been thus misplaced and to that extent we have let them down.

Moreover, when we express pleasure at the increased scope for our exports, let us always remember that, contrary to the increase claimed by a recent broadcast, the real value of our money incomes has been reduced and is likely to be reduced. We shall certainly find this when we travel abroad, if we attempt to go tomorrow. We shall certainly find it when the inevitable rises in the cost of living at home have begun to take place. Nor do I think that there is any reason to expect diplomatic benefit from what has happened. I suggest that we fool ourselves if we think that what has happened will make any impression on those abroad who are implacably resolved to extract the last ounce of humiliation from their late comrades in war.

Having said that, I must confess that I cannot associate myself with those who put all the blame on the present Government. In spite of what has been said this afternoon, I myself believe that the claim is true that in 1964 they inherited a bad situation. It is possible, I agree, that this situation might have been handled with more firmness by an alternative government, but those who argue that such a government could have ridden out that crisis, with an overheated and over-extended economy, without an abrupt change of policy, fail to convince me. I think that they cherish a most dangerous delusion.

I also think it is true that after a period of (how shall I put it tactfully?) some infirmity of purpose, the present Government, in July, 1966, imposed restraints which no former government had succeeded in imposing. I hasten to say that I do not think that the present Government's general economic policy has in other ways been such as to reassure business and promote enterprise—quite the contrary. But I am inclined to believe that

17

there is at least something in the claim that on this occasion there has been particularly bad luck. It was not long after the imposition of the July measures that demand in continental Europe began to undergo some recession, and the economy of the United States went into a condition which is described over there as a 'pause'. Nor, surely, should we underestimate the effect on confidence in the pound of the troubles in the Middle East, the closing of the Suez Canal and the dock strike, for which, after all, the Government cannot be held to be responsible. I also think it is only right to say that the present Chancellor of the Exchequer has defended an unpopular policy with great courage and has argued his case like a man. Therefore, although I am opposed root and branch to many of his policies, I feel very sorry for him in his present position, and I personally hope that he will not feel obliged to resign until the rest of his companions resign, too.

Be that as it may, I am bound to say that in the circumstances that had developed by last week, last Saturday's decision seems to me to have been unavoidable. I think that in those circumstances it would have been wrong to run still further into debt in what would probably has been a vain attempt to cope with a loss of confidence in sterling which had piled up. It would have been wrong to have burdened our future for a chance which was intrinsically so precarious. In those circumstances, I think that we had to devalue. But I do not rejoice in the decision and, contrary to some authorities, I do not regard it as a prelude to an easy time.

The great question is: will it work? And the answer, I suggest, is that it all depends: it all depends on policy. In spite of the slight doubts which have been insinuated by the noble Viscount, Lord Eccles, I know no serious reason to suppose that in the present circumstances of the world, with our present prices what they are compared with prices in the rest of the world at the new exchange rate, this degree of devaluation should not do the trick and bring our balance of payments into equilibrium again, always provided that it is not offset by inflation of prices and incomes at home. I am equally sure that if it is so offset, it will not work; still more, if ham-handed financial measures blunt the incentives of the new exchange rate— for example, an increase in corporation profits tax. If that is so, then we shall soon be where we were before. We shall be in the position in which France was before the advent of de Gaulle. We shall be like some Latin American Republic, staggering on from one humiliating crisis to another and destroying civic virtue and self-respect in the process. So that in the last analysis the question is a question of nerve and clarity of purpose.

In conclusion, may I utter a word of warning? We shall not solve our troubles by mere exhortation, by phrase-making on television like 'modernisation of the economy', of which no one really knows the concrete significance, and which sounds hollower and hollower every time it is uttered. Nor should we rely on vague talk about incomes policy. Of course there must be an incomes policy in the public sector. If there is not, there is chaos. Of course we must hope that responsible trade union leaders will bear in mind the national interest in putting forward their claims. But—and this surely is all-important—they are not likely to be able to restrain their followers if there is a general inflationary tendency abroad. The trade unions would have to be staffed by archangels to exercise self-restraint in such circumstances, and neither Mr Cousins nor anyone else in that area is an archangel.

The more one thinks about the present situation, the more one is forced to the conclusion that there is no excuse for the Government to shuffle off responsibility on to anybody else. There will be no excuse if the Government stifle export incentives by unwise tax measures. There will be no excuse if they do not reduce expenditure. There will be no excuse if they do not keep firm control of the credit base. I am not clear that this is as generally appreciated as it should be. Public finance and the volume of money are the instruments which are ultimately at the Government's disposal. The nation will watch very anxiously to see how they are used. And all of us should examine our heads and hearts to see if our criteria and our aims are clear. We must surely all beware at this time lest we fall into the frame of mind described in Arnold's famous poem 'Empedocles on Etna':

We want all pleasant ends, but will use no harsh means.

5 The U.S. Deficit and the International Problem

Motion: The Economic Situation; 10 April 1968

My Lords, I am in substantial agreement with the general contention that, other things being equal, and at any rate from the purely technical point of view, the present prospects of our economy may be regarded as considerably more hopeful than they have been in the recent past. Whatever we may think of the responsibility for the events leading up to devaluation—and I adhere to the view that, at any rate from July 1966, onwards, the Government had very bad luck in that respect—I suspect that we should all agree that the fact of devaluation is providing a useful stimulus to export. I know that appearances are somewhat deceptive. Because of the rise in the cost of certain imported materials and the abolition of export rebates, the magnitude of the advantage of devaluation is exaggerated by the percentage change in the rate. But when all account has been taken of the necessary subtractions, there still remains in many fields an advantage of perhaps between 8 and 9 per cent. And if the pressure of domestic demand is sufficiently restrained, this should surely prove a powerful influence to introducing a balance-of-payments surplus.

Now that the Budget has at last been produced, we have some assurance that the restraint on demand is going to happen. I still wish that some gesture of this sort—the immediate application of the regulator, for instance—could have taken place on the morrow of devaluation. The public would have taken anything in those weeks; and the position of the pound in the foreign exchanges would have been powerfully strengthened.

But in spite of its sins of retrospection and Mr Jenkins' somewhat unworthy sneer at top managers who provide for retirement by saving, I should not wish to withhold great admiration from his general conception. He certainly can claim that at least we have measures which do not err on the side of caution in imposing the necessary constraints. I do not go any of the way with those who argue that he could safely have done less, and I do not think that we should fail to render tribute to what I persist in regarding as an act of considerable political courage which, from the technical point of view, at any rate, meets the requirements of the situation. Needless to say, I do not doubt the desirability of further scrutiny of public expenditure; but I suspect that this involves time and perhaps a radical reformulation of certain conceptions of public service. I think it would have been unreasonable to ask this of Mr Jenkins in the short time in which he has occupied his important office.

Still concentrating on the purely domestic situation, I think it seems fairly clear that the main danger remaining is the danger of renewed inflation of costs by run-away increases of the wage and salary level. There is no doubt that this is well recognised by the Government, who, as we all know, are running into severe difficulties with some of their supporters in providing safeguards against this contingency. Incidentally, I should like to express some admiration for Mr Jenkins' candour in making it clear that this is a situation in which it is positively desirable that, for the time being, in order to restrain consumption, prices should rise faster than money incomes. But I hope very much that in seeking to deal with this matter the Government will not rely exclusively on any form of incomes policy. Even after the discussion that has taken place, I cannot help thinking that this is a matter on which a great deal of confusion still persists.

Let me guard myself against misunderstanding in this connection. I have no doubt at all that the Government must have an incomes policy in regard to the public sector. After all, the Government is the employer there and unless it has a policy concerning its demand for labour this important section of the economy must remain in sheer confusion. Nor should I wish to deny that policies of freeze or semi-freeze in the economy as a whole are necessarily ineffective in the very short run. I think experience shows that they are not easy to enforce and that the longer they are resorted to the more resistance they encounter. But I do not doubt, without in the least abdicating my position as a lover of freedom, that in periods of great emergency, if the co-operation of the trade unions and employers can be secured, such policies may have a useful stabilising influence. I do, however, doubt very much whether it is wise to rely on their effectiveness for any but a comparatively short period. They generate anomalies while they last: what is more, when they cease to operate they run the danger of leaving behind them banked-up demands which eventually bring about a situation not very different from that which they were set up to avoid. Indeed it is difficult to be sure that with a policy of freeze or semi-freeze limited to a year or eighteen months, the eventual rise in costs will be much less than it would have been if there had been no such policy.

Hence, my Lords, I submit that it is of paramount importance to make the main aim of policy not the control of incomes but the control of aggregate expenditure. And here I should like to emphasise the impor-tance of not overlooking the part that can be played in this respect by proper regulation of the credit base. I know that there are those whose views deserve respect who consider that attention to the movements of the quantity of money is an obsolete preoccupation. I know that it is fashionable in some quarters to regard the fluctuation of the credit base as being necessarily and desirably passive to the needs of trade. But I very much doubt the wisdom of this attitude. I certainly should not wish to be understood to be arguing that monetary policy alone is capable of exercising a sufficient control of the volume of aggregate expenditure, and I know few at the present day who would maintain such a position. But I would urge that it would be unwise to leave that out or to ignore the very powerful assistance it can render.

So much as regards domestic policy and its prospects, other things being equal. But now we are in a situation in which other things are not likely to be equal and domestic policy is not likely to be able to dominate the situation, however much it may seek to influence it. We are in the grip of tremendous events in the world at large, many of which are outside our power of control, and prediction in such circumstances is almost anybody's guess. But perhaps I may be allowed to make one or two general remarks— not predictions—which represent my own effort to see the position in some sort of perspective.

First of all, it seems to me important to realise that our troubles are not due to any lack of world liquidity in the recent past. Indeed, there has been no lack of such liquidity since the end of the war: look at what has happened to the value of money. Everywhere during this period there has been a most considerable rise of prices. In such circumstances it seems to me to be impossible reasonably to contend that there has been too little general liquidity in the world at large: rather I would urge that there has been too much. In the future, I agree the picture begins to appear different. A little way ahead we probably walk through the looking glass, so to speak, and find ourselves confronted with a real problem of this sort. That is, of course, the *raison d'être* for all the work which has been done recently by the Group of Ten and others, on the institution of Special Drawing Rights at the International Monetary Fund.

No, my Lords, the main cause of the recent gold crisis has been not the absence of general liquidity but the growing deficit in the United States balance of payments. Needless to say, the operation of this cause has been vastly reinforced by apprehensions and rumours of a possible change in the price of gold. But ultimately it is the United States deficit wich is responsible. Doubtless it is true that this deficit does not spring from any very fundamental malaise in the United States economy. The entire deficit is fractional in regard to the United States gross national product. It has not been, as ours has been, a deficit on current account; it is essentially a deficit on capital account due to what, having regard to the United States' present external earning capacity, has been excessive investment abroad, foreign aid and war expenditure—causes much more susceptible to control than more deep-seated maladies. Nevertheless, this deficit on capital account has given rise to a shrinkage in the United States' gold reserve; and this shrinkage has been serious and growing.

Such a state of affairs inevitably arouses international apprehensions. It is true that these apprehensions have been heightened by propaganda emanating in certain high quarters in Continental Europe. But if there had been none of this, the apprehensions would still have grown. There was, of course, a time in the early fifties when an increase in the dollar holding was positively preferred by many Continental central banks. But recently such increases have encountered more and more reluctance; and, it must be admitted, understandably so. After all, however much we may deplore the attitude of the French Government to Allies who once helped to deliver them from servitude under the Nazis, their analysis is logically correct when they argue that holding increasing amounts of dollars is, in effect, making loans to the United States. And it is clear that from their point of view this is not necessarily a desirable state of affairs.

Such a situation was surely bound to lead to trouble sooner or later; and it must be admitted that such trouble has been predicted in many quarters. Whatever we may think of his views with regard to the desirability of a rehabilitation of the old-fashioned gold standard, it must be put to the credit of Monsieur Rueff that, in season and out of season, he has pointed to the latent dangers in the present workings of the post-war gold exchange standard and the enormous volume of free dollar holdings abroad. I should like to add that, although in the end I do not support Monsieur Rueff's proposals for the reform of the international monetary system, I know from long personal acquaintance that he at least is not an enemy of the English-speaking world; and it can be cited as a proof of this that his plan for the adjustment of the price of gold carried with it a generous provision for easing the burden on the reserve centres concerned of the sterling and dollar balances.

Now, as I see things, this crisis is not one which can be cured by the mere institution of Special Drawing Rights at the International Monetary Fund. I hasten to say that I approve of this plan. I hope that it will be possible to bring it into being. But it is essentially a plan for easing the general liquidity situation in the future. Even if it could be brought into being immediately, its chances of survival would be small indeed if the United States balance of payments continued to be adverse. It might help for a time, but in the end people would no more be willing to accumulate paper claims on the International Monetary Fund than they would be to accumulate dollars.

But equally, in my judgment, the underlying situation is not to be cured by a change in the price of gold. I am not against such a change in all circumstances, although if it were to take place at present I should be extremely apprehensive of its inflationary potentialities. But, so far as the present unbalance is concerned, all that it could do would be to provide a further breathing space in which measures might be taken to alleviate the deficit on the United States balance of payments. If this deficit persists, then, even if there has been a change in the price of gold, there will still eventually arrive an ultimate breakdown of the dollar exchange.

In the end, it seems to me, there are only two possible solutions. The first is some contraction of United States' expenditure, either at home or abroad, or both. I do not myself believe that this need be very severe, especially if, as might be hoped, it were accompanied by expansion on the part of countries at present in surplus. But I am afraid that, so far as we are concerned, it certainly will not make things easier. Failing this, however, the alternative is a total demonetisation of gold, at any rate for the time being, by the United States' authorities, and a freeing of restrictions on movements of the dollar in the exchange market. If one likes to put it that way one can describe this as letting the dollar float.

Such a solution has some attractions in pure theory; and, let us not deceive ourselves, there are now many high authorities in America who support it. But it seems to me that it is likely in practice to be attended by many unwished-for complications. In the first place, it is very unlikely that the financial authorities elsewhere would all be willing to see the dollar fluctuate in terms of their own money. They would therefore hitch on to the dollar in some way or other and maintain fixity of exchange rates therewith. It seems to me probable that we ourselves should feel impelled to do this, and I am sure that quite a number of other centres would do likewise.

In such a state of affairs the centres which continued to maintain the old parity with gold would be at an increasing disadvantage in markets in which their producers were in competition with members of the Dollar Group, as were members of the old Gold Block in the years following President Roosevelt's experiment with adjustable dollar rates. The probability is, therefore, that they would be tempted to devaluations in terms of gold, and this in turn would easily lead to further depreciation of the floating dollar and associated currencies. It might come out all right in the end, but it seems likely to me that it would give rise to a period of financial anarchy and confusion which would do good to very few of us.

At the moment, the position is that the central bankers have attempted to stave off ultimate decisions by setting up a two-tier system in which gold transfers among themselves take place at existing parities but the private gold market is free. And so far this system has been effective; the price of gold in the free market has fallen from the levels it attained at the height of the crisis. But one is bound to ask oneself: How long can this situation last? Doubtless if there is a real prospect of reduction in the United States deficit, then the free market price of gold will fall, the gap will be closed, and the necessity for these exceptional measures may disappear. But if there is no such prospect, then nothing can be more certain than a period of greater and greater strain. The temptation on the other central bankers to make a profit on their increasing gold holdings must eventually become very great indeed, and in the next crisis a two-tier system will no longer be available.

What will actually happen? Frankly, my Lords, I do not know. So much in the present situation depends on attitudes and policies whose occurrence and influence is anybody's guess. But of one thing I am certain: that for us the supreme need is to keep our own house in order and to support whatever measures are necessary to achieve this end. Any relaxation in such circumstances can only make the situation worse both for us and for the world at large.

6 Disaster Averted but Apprehensions Continue

Finance Bill Second Reading and Remaining Stages; 17 July 1968

My Lords, I agree with what speakers favourable to the Government have said, in this Chamber and elsewhere, that the news from Basle and the improvement in the trade figures are grounds for some satisfaction. But before we follow Mr Aubrey Jones—or more exalted authorities—in talking of economic miracles, I think we should recognise, in the interests of realism, that all that has happened so far is that the situation has been prevented from becoming worse. Whatever may be the extent of our deliverance in the future, we are still months, even years, away from a state of affairs which can be free from deep anxieties.

Let us take the Basle agreements, or what we know of them at present. It is indeed very good news that the danger of massive withdrawals of the sterling balances seems to have been averted, and I am sure that the gratitude of us all is due to that great and good man, the Governor of the Bank of England, for the ceaseless and dedicated labours which have brought this about. In my opinion, we do not pay sufficient tribute to the men like Sir Leslie O'Brien and his illustrious predecessor, the noble Earl, Lord Cromer, who by their vigilance and shining integrity have sustained our financial reputation in quarters which have power to help at a time when there was some reason to fear that that reputation was in danger.

But what has happened is essentially that a great disaster has been prevented. If, without support from elsewhere, there had been withdrawal on a large scale of funds hitherto held in London by the central banks of the sterling area, nothing could have prevented a catastrophic fall in the external value of the pound, with all the internal damage and international chaos that that would have involved. But there is nothing in what has happened which positively improves our position on current account. There is nothing which finances the present deficit. And if the transfers take place, and our obligations to pay in sterling are transformed into debts to members of the Bank for International Settlements, then in the long run the burden on the balance of payments may be actually increased by obligations of repayment which might not otherwise have taken place. There is not much cause for jubilation here, but some cause for quiet thankfulness.

The improvement in the trade figures, especially the drop in imports, is indeed more positively relevant. If it persists, it will certainly be an indication that the devaluation is beginning to work and that internal policy is at last on the right lines. But how premature to proclaim recovery! We are still running a deficit on current account. At the present rate of recovery it is difficult to believe that we shall be breaking even much before the end of the year. As has been said already, if we are to repay the debts which we have incurred recently, still more if we are to accumulate reserves adequate to the business of a great industrial and financial nation, we shall have to run surpluses of at least £400 million a year for years to come. I do not suggest that this is impossible. When one looks around and sees what has occurred in other centres, such as Germany or Italy, which 20 years ago were in a much worse position than we are now, it is clear that it can be done. But it is early days to speak as if it were far on the way. Many years of effort and restraint lie ahead, and at the present time—let us face it—we are still in a position of danger.

In this connection, my Lords, it is worth remembering the narrowness of the margin available. The devaluation was comparatively small. I am not arguing that it should have been greater. I still find it difficult to believe that, given proper internal restraint, the pound was greatly overvalued; and since we were not accompanied downwards by many other centres, as happened in 1949, the cutting edge of what has happened, so to speak, is very extensive. But when due account has been taken of increased costs of imported raw materials, the abolition of export rebates and so on, the advantage to our exports cannot be much more than 10 per cent, if that. It would not take much internal inflation to wipe that out, and to sustain a disposition to import far beyond our present means. It is clear, then, that it is overwhelmingly important that the rate of spending in general, both internally and externally, shall not run ahead of what we can afford; in particular, that incomes shall not rise faster than productivity, and that consumption shall be so restrained as to allow appropriate internal investment and the creation of an external surplus.

My Lords, this brings me to the occasion for to-day's debate—the Finance Bill and its implications. Let me say at once that I am in broad sympathy both with its aims and with its methods. This is not to say that I think that our system of public finance is in a particularly healthy state. I think it has been ailing for some time—longer than the term of office of the present Government—both on the side of expenditure and on the side of taxation; and I certainly think that its ailments have been increased by some measures introduced by the present Government—the capital gains tax without an index number clause, corporations profit tax, and S.E.T.

The immediate need of the situation this spring was a drastic curtailment of consumption; and I agree that, given the instruments at his disposal, the Chancellor has done the right thing to get it. I have not much use for the so-called once-for-all special levy: it will not raise a great deal of money and it will impose special burdens on some who have provided for retirement. But if it was the political price for an otherwise sensible policy, perhaps it was not too much to pay. The main tendency to shift to some extent to indirect taxation seems to me in present circumstances to be wholly welcome. Admirers of the communist system will note that, in spite of some inequality of income, the main instrument of taxation in Soviet Russia is a turnover tax. In this respect, I submit, the Chancellor has done a wise and courageous thing.

Nevertheless, I submit that we should deceive ourselves if we were to regard the present situation in this respect as entirely satisfactory; if we were to think that, so far as public finance is concerned, all that needs to be done now is to sit back and wait for an economic miracle. I think that much needs to be done to improve our system of taxation, both in respect of incentive and in respect of justice. I think, too, that not nearly enough has been done to restrain the growth of public expenditure. In this connection I do not wish to give countenance to the vulgar view that within the limits of present policies there are vast areas of waste to be remedied by immediate economies. I mean rather that there are, in my judgment, large fields of expenditure where we need rethinking of fundamental policies— areas of outlay where more selective expenditure would allow at once more to be given to the really poor but less given to others not in need.

Much more immediate is concern for the present volume of spending. In spite of the Budget, and in spite of some reduction in sales in some shops, it seems to me that the disposition to spend is still too high for our present state of convalescence. Taxation or no taxation, too many people have got into the habit of preferring consumption goods to reasonable liquidity and investment. This tendency was already widespread because of continuing inflation; but it has certainly been considerably strengthened by the long delay in introducing the post-devaluation Budget.

With great respect and admiration for the present Chancellor of the Exchequer, I have racked my brains to discover valid grounds for his failure to act earlier; but I have found none. Why on earth did he hold his hand? In the weeks following devaluation this people would have taken anything in the nature of restraint and austerity. As it was, as has been said already in the debate, the delay gave rise to a vast orgy of spending, which must be held largely responsible for the uncertainty regarding the future of sterling which has persisted ever since. Even now I doubt whether the habits thus engendered have been fully abandoned. 'After us the deluge' is still too much the prevailing mood in many quarters.

In this connection, I believe that far too little attention has been given by this or earlier Governments to effective encouragement of saving. We all know that saving is not something that you encourage in the depths of depression. But I imagine that most of us would agree that, at any rate during the last 20 years, the tasks of all governments in this country would have been materially eased had the disposition to save been greater. One of the main reasons why this was not so was, of course, the fact of inflation itself. If the value of money is falling, as it has been falling pretty consistently since the war—under Conservative governments as well as under Labour governments—then even high rates of interest may not be a sufficient compensation for the loss of purchasing power; and sooner or later people find this out.

This frame of mind cannot be wholly eradicated while the expectation of inflation persists. But I suggest that far more could be done than has yet been done to reverse the tendency. The tax system as we have it at present positively discriminates against savings: it taxes the incomes out of which savings are made, and it taxes the incomes which they reap; and it adds insult to injury by designating as 'unearned income' what a man receives from the provision he has made against retirement. I strongly commend to the Chancellor the serious consideration of measures to rectify this anomaly, and if he has any trouble with the theory involved there is an excellent book by a Mr Nicholas Kaldor which, in this respect at any rate, would be very helpful to him.

7 Lessons from Experience and Warnings for the Future

Debate on the Address (Second Day); 7 July 1970

My Lords, the subject of to-day's debate raises questions relating both to the past and to the future, both to what has happened and to what may happen. As regards the past, as a cross-bencher I profoundly desire to avoid party recriminations. I do not think that such recriminations help much in understanding the difficult problems with which we are faced. But I do believe that there have been errors in the past on both sides, and I think that there is some purpose to be served in attempting to draw some lessons therefrom. I have three such lessons particularly in mind.

Thus the first: if we go back to the years before the late Administration took over, I think it is clear from that experience that, if there is any danger to the balance of payments, to make a dash for freedom in the hope that an increased production will take you over the hump is very dangerous indeed. I do not question the good will of the policies of that period, but, equally, I do not doubt that these policies did leave an extremely difficult problem to those who inherited them. Perhaps it was talked about too much, but that is another story.

My second point is that if you inherit a balance of payments problem, if you do not intend to devalue you must make sure that your internal policies are sufficiently tough to restore the position at the old rate of exchange. I still think that in 1964 there was no need to devalue, and I respect the motives which led to the decision at that time to retain the old parity. But I also think that until 1966, when it was certainly getting very late, the policies adopted were very inadequate for that purpose. In 1966 things were different. I think the policies then adopted might have been adequate had it not been for considerable external bad luck and eventually the shipping strike—one of the very few strikes in my lifetime which can be said to have done really serious damage to the economy.

Thirdly, once you have decided to devalue, as we did in 1967, you cannot afford to delay for more than a few days or weeks the stiffening of fiscal and monetary policy which is necessary if the devalued exchange is not itself to be an aggravating factor. This especially, my Lords, if you tell

30

the public that the money in its pockets has not lost any power to purchase. I think that the delay from December of that year until the normal Budget time, the delay of appropriate tax policies, was a mistake; still more the failure at once to impose strict control on the supply of money. After that, however, not perhaps without some tactful prodding from the authorities at the I.M.F., the correct medicine was administered; and I think Mr Jenkins and his colleagues in the late Government might indeed claim considerable credit for vindicating expectations emanating from elementary economic theory. We are not out of the wood yet, my Lords, not by any means; but certainly some progress has been made.

Turning from the lessons of the past to the prospects of the future, I see two sets of problems; connected perhaps, but sufficiently distinct to be capable of disentanglement; problems of general financial policy and problems of immediate action. As regards general policy, I have little doubt that some of the measures of recent years have left the tax system in a terrible mess—S.E.T., capital gains tax; corporation profits tax. Frankly, my Lords, S.E.T. is a monstrosity with its absurd discriminations. Only a mind insulated from reality by a very amiable disposition to excessive intellectual acrobatics could have thought of it. I hasten to add that I hope that the Chancellor in one of his more Messianic moods will not try to remedy things by simple repeal; releasing some hundreds of millions of pounds of additional purchasing power. Better, I suggest, for the time being to turn it into an overall payroll tax, without exceptions and capable of rapid adjustment up and down to meet the needs of the changing situation. Better, at any rate, until we know what we have to do if we succeed in getting into the Common Market.

To the capital gains tax, my Lords, I have no objection whatever in principle; but while it remains without an index number provision then in times of inflation it is, *inter alia*, an annual capital levy, with all the disincentive to saving and prudence which that sort of tax implies. You put your money into equities; the price level rises 10 per cent, and the price level of equities may rise 10 per cent or it may not. But if it does then, low and behold! you are taxed—although the real value of your capital has remained constant. Why Mr Callaghan, who is a humane and honourable man, should have countenanced such an anomaly in his measure passes my comprehension.

As to the corporation profits tax, perhaps the least said the better. I learned my public finance from a great teacher of economics, not popular on one side of the House, the late Hugh Dalton. He taught me that taxes on company profits, as distinct from taxes on individual incomes, were both inequitable and uneconomic. I think it was a great pity that, at a time when in other parts of the world people were getting tired of this sort of thing, we should have landed ourselves with this thoroughly reactionary measure which will take years and years to unscramble.

Then, my Lords, beyond all the troubles created by particular measures there is the general problem of the very considerable disincentive created by the excessive weight of marginal taxation of incomes. I know that the existence of such a disincentive effect is disputed—and I do not need to be reminded that some of the finest work in the world is completely uninfluenced by pecuniary considerations. But I know, too, that the impulses of many ordinary men and women are so influenced, and I think that it is wisdom to legislate for a community of middling motivation rather than for a community of Franciscan idealists. We should all agree, surely, that a marginal tax rate of 20s. in the pound would have a dampening effect upon effort. Why should the dampening effect cease if it is 19s. or 18s. 6d.? I suggest that something ought to be done about this; and in my judgment it would be a good thing if it were laid down that rates should be such that no man should be penalised by the loss of more than, let us say, 50 per cent of his income. But all such changes of general policy need time and prudence.

Meanwhile, the present situation, if not immediately catastrophic, is sufficiently disturbing. In recent months the income inflation in this country has been at the rate of something in the neighbourhood of 10 per cent, against a growth rate which just recently has not been very much above zero. This situation simply must not continue. And it is no use trying to shrug it off by saying that other countries also are inflating. I doubt very much whether many are inflating so much against so small a growth rate, and if they are not then it is only a matter of time—it may be some time; I hope it is—before we have further external difficulties. But even if we are all going up at the same rate, the fact of absolute, as distinct from relative, inflation would still be incompatible with distributive justice and economic stability.

As regards distributive justice, inflation means that all with fixed incomes are penalised: pensioners, owners of Government and fixed-interest bearing securities, all whose salaries or wages are adjusted only at long intervals. I know it is sometimes said that this can all be put right by more frequent adjusting. Very well. But, if that is said, let us not forget that the adjustment, to be just, must be continuous; and if the adjustment is continuous, the inflation loses all its stimulus. If all incomes and prices go up together, the net effect is just like adding noughts to all the figures in the account books, or altering the accounting from, shall we say, Arabic to Roman numerals. As to stability—I say it without exaggeration—if this sort of thing gathers momentum, I do not see how it can be stopped without shocks to expectations which may have very serious consequences. Our whole system is getting geared up to non-stop inflation—witness the present level of interest rates. Do we really think that eliminating this is something that can be done without trouble?

What then are we to do? I should have thought that another wage freeze was not 'on', at any rate for the time being. A large section of opinion, some of which I respect, still clings to the idea of a permanent incomes policy—

P.I.B. for ever. I confess to doubts about this. Of course there must be a public incomes policy, otherwise the Government, as employer, is not discharging its duty in that respect. If the Government is not willing occasionally to say, 'Thus far shalt thou go and no farther', what are we to expect of employers in the private sector? I submit that we have seen the disadvantages of this quite often recently.

But elsewhere, outside the public sector, throughout the rest of the economy, it is not at all clear to me that long-run success is to be expected from this sort of policy. Indeed, my fear is that the remedy may prove as bad as the disease. I doubt very much—I say it with trepidation—whether in recent years the P.I.B. did very much to restrain inflation. I would go further and say that I suspect that the setting of norms, so-called, may in fact have made things worse and prompted claims that might otherwise have been more moderate. Anyway, it is clear to me that, as a permanent long-run policy, control of prices and incomes from the centre can work effectively only with much more interference with individual liberty, and much more control from the centre than the majority of this people are as yet prepared to put up with. I find it a significant circumstance that the resistance to this idea comes quite as much from the majority of moderate and helpful trade union leaders as from any who might be farther to the Left.

Whatever emergency measures may be forced upon us—and we are moving in very unknown waters at the moment—in my judgment the time has come to return fundamentally to the original conception of stabilisation policy. Agreed that the Government has a duty to provide against deflation and mass unemployment. We all agree about that. But it should also be agreed that it has no duty to provide the money to finance inflation. It must not be committed to a full employment policy, whatever the demands on the gross national product may be in the shape of claims for increased incomes. That way lies eventual hyper-inflation.

The Government should be prepared to say to all concerned, 'We undertake, either by fiscal means or by monetary means'—and I am an eclectic in this respect—'to endeavour to maintain such a volume of aggregate demand as will sustain reasonably high employment at income rates rising with productivity; but, beyond that, we are not prepared to provide the money. This is the point at which you, individuals and organisations with dispersed initiative, must choose. It is not for us—the Government—to be forced into steps which lower the value of money and penalise all with fixed incomes.'

Some may say that this is an impossible conception for a modern democratic community. I agree that so far since the war there has been very little on these lines, under any Government, at any rate in this country. But consider the alternatives: either total control of incomes, leading to a good deal of control of almost everything, or continuing inflation and all that that implies. My Lords, I suggest that we have to talk this out in a grown-up way, and I have yet to be convinced that among this people, if such talk takes place, reason and persuasion have not some chance in the end.

Meanwhile, in conclusion, may I venture to express the hope that the Chancellor will eschew the siren voices suggesting yet a further stimulus to aggregate demand while incomes are still rising faster than productivity. It may be that the income inflation has gone so far that a total and immediate application of the brakes would be unwise. There are grave international liquidity problems hovering around. But let no one think that in our present position the utmost prudence is not necessary when contemplating this kind of stimulus. It is often said—it is a commonplace of uninformed discussion—that if only production is stimulated enough, nothing more is needed. In my opinion, my Lords, this is just wishful thinking. I agree, of course, that if production could be so increased as to bridge the gap between a 10 per cent increase of incomes and, say, a one per cent rate of growth, this would be all right. But does any serious-minded person think that that is immediately possible? How agreeable it would be for us all if things were as simple as that!

8 A Fool's Paradise—the Vulnerability of the Government

Motion: Public Spending and Economic Policy; 18 November 1970

My Lords, there are elements in the Government's policy with which I profoundly agree, but there are also elements—or, at least, the appearance of elements—which fill me with some apprehension.

Let me begin with what I can agree with, although I have the fear that this will make noble Lords on the Opposition benches less inclined to believe my credentials when I come to the disapprobatory grounds. I welcome in principle, if not always in detail, the introduction of greater selectivity in the administration of benefits. I have never been able to see why large numbers of people should receive benefits which they could perfectly afford for themselves. I agree, too, with the diminution of various subsidies to industry. There may be exceptions for defence industries, depressed areas and the like, but as a first approximation I am sure it is a good principle that economic activities, State-owned or otherwise, should be made to stand on their own feet. I approve, too, of the general attitude of ministers that the scope of government has become too large for efficiency and should be diminished where it is sensible and practical to do so—which does not mean, my Lords, that I think that the functions of government are those of the night watchman. But having said that, I must also say that much of this, although commendable in itself, is almost totally irrelevant to the main problem of the moment—the problem of continuing inflation. The last position I should wish to occupy is that of panic-monger, but I am sincerely alarmed at the present situation, which in my judgment is certainly at once the most serious and the most intractable problem with which we have been confronted since the war.

I think experience shows that you can live with a rate of inflation of, perhaps, 2 per cent or even 3 per cent, although cumulatively, in the absence of adjustments, this bears hardly on the more sober and prudent members of the community. But the rate at which we are inflating at the moment—a percentage rate of increase of wages of over 12 per cent per annum and of growth of not much more than 2 per cent—is different. Such

35

an inflation undermines the whole basis of business calculation, of depreciation allowances; it involves the most blatant and cruel distributive injustice, even if there are biennial reviews of pensions and such like; and it eventually, as we know from history, creates an economic and a political atmosphere inimical to soical peace, to mutual understanding and, eventually, to common honesty. I do not know any example in history in which an inflation of this order which has been allowed to go on for very long, has been stopped, as eventually it must be, without severe dislocation and hardship one way or the other. It is possible that there may yet be time for us to escape from these consequences. I pray that it may be so, but the sands are running out.

My Lords, the taunts of the Opposition on this matter leave me cold—very cold. The late Government bequeathed to their successors a crisis which in my judgment is worse than the crisis which their predecessors bequeathed to them, and, as they have often emphasised, that was bad enough. It is quite true that, as a result of devaluation and a temporary exercise of prudence in fiscal and monetary policy, there has been an alleviation of our difficulties with the balance of payments. Let there be credit where credit is due. But the abandonment of any attempt to control the causes making for inflation has created a problem far worse than the balance-of-payments problem. That, after all, was soluble—an adjustment of the rate of exchange and a firm control of the money supply. It was soluble without much hardship to anybody. But an internal inflation of the kind from which we are suffering now, if it goes on, will create hardship for most of us.

Let there be no mistake about what is happening and what has happened. We all know about the bargains in the labour market, and I do not want to discuss that further. But how few realise that, in the quarter before the election, the money supply was increasing, not at the target rate set by the Chancellor, but at the rate of 16 per cent per annum. Let me be clear, my Lords: I am accusing nobody. Mr Jenkins is a very honourable man. I do not believe that he deliberately threw the reins on the horse's neck. The authorities of the Bank, with whom I have the greatest sympathy, are dedicated to the public interest. I have no doubt at all that what happened was the by-product not of intention but, as so many untoward events in this world are, of muddle and confusion of purpose. The fact is that under the last Government the funds were being created which will be sustaining the inflationary pressure for months to come.

If I am not impressed by the indignation of the Opposition at the situation which they have passed on, I am equally not impressed by the spirit in which, in public at least, the present Government are confronting the problems to which it gives rise. I have said already that I approve of the policy of less government in the sphere of industrial operations. But I do not approve of less government where the value of money is concerned. I know no responsible economist of any school of thought who believes that with a paper standard, the standard that we have at present and certainly will have in future, the Government have not the most momentous responsibilities of control. There can be no *laissez-faire* as regards aggregate demand. Yet it sometimes almost seems as if Ministers believe that there can be; that if they reform the law relating to trade unions, diminish the disincentives to initiative and reform an admittedly ridiculous tax system, they will have done all that it is reasonable to expect of them, that there will be a glorious increase of production and that inflation will die away, if not of its own accord because of a new spirit.

My Lords, this is a tragic delusion. Just as the Labour Government seemed to believe at first that the 1964 exchange crisis could be dealt with by mainly socialist measures, so the Conservatives seem to think that the present crisis can be dealt with mainly by individualist measures. But in fact neither meets the problem. I can believe that if the disparity between the growth rate and the inflation rate was of the order of 2 per cent, then perhaps some abolition of the more obvious restrictions on enterprise and some greater order in industrial relations might perhaps bring about a rate of increase of production sufficient to bridge the gap. It was for that reason that yesterday I addressed a question on this matter to the noble Earl sitting on the front bench. I wondered how much he thought that production would increase as a result of the beneficial measures now being introduced. In my own judgment, my Lords, the gap is not of that order. In my judgment, we are living in a fool's paradise if we suppose that the measures of the mini-Budget and the proposed industrial relations legislation can stop the inflation. I say that it is an abdication of responsibility to stop there, and an abdication for which history will provide no excuse.

What then are we to do? I can well understand the reluctance of the Government to countenance the idea of a general freeze of prices and incomes; although if they go on without firmer policies they may well have to change their minds. I agree with what was said yesterday by the noble Lord, Lord Thorneycroft, that no policy should be ruled out *a priori* at this stage. But, quite apart from election promises, which we all know can be broken at least as decently as rash promises to get married, a general freeze, if it goes on for very long, begins to make rogues of us all. Consider the situation. As a manufacturer I am forbidden, whatever is happening to my costs—and I am talking about a general freeze—to advance the price of commodity 'A'. What do I do? I lower its quality or I turn to the production of commodity 'B', which is not yet on the market and which consequently does not come into the schedule. Or—to turn to labour relations—my best expert in a certain field comes to me and tells me that he has been offered £500 a year more by my chief industrial rival. 'I'm sorry, old chap,' I reply. 'I must not give you a rise in your present position. But I have been thinking for some time that we need to fill a job with some different title. If you are willing to take that, then I think we could legitimately pay you £1,000 a year more than you are getting in your present one'. My Lords, do you think that this is fanciful? I ask all of you who have knowledge of affairs if that is not a typical temptation under any wage and prices freeze which goes on for very long.

Well, then, what about an orderly incomes policy? I well understand the theory underlying this demand and I wholeheartedly respect the impulse towards it. If he were here I should like to say that, much as I have suffered from his tongue and his pen in the last 25 years, I greatly respect the courage with which the noble Lord, Lord Balogh, has often spoken (in defiance of the inclinations of many sitting on his own benches) in favour of this policy. But it is one thing to demand such a policy; it is quite another thing to spell out the way in which to execute it. Suppose we tell the Coal Board that it will not be allowed to put up its prices or to borrow to finance an increased wage of so much per cent. Is that an acceptable incomes policy? Well, since the Government, willy nilly, are involved in the Coal Board, I should certainly find it part of an acceptable incomes policy.

But, my Lords, the logic of general regulation, the regulation of incomes throughout the whole system, carries you into very deep waters indeed. Even at the height of the war crisis, that great national leader, Ernie Bevin, refused to undertake the detailed regulation of wage bargains. I believe it would be an exaggeration to say that under the last Government, inspired by the best will in the world, the operations of the Prices and Incomes Board restrained the rise of incomes by more than a negligible percentage. I am bound to say, having searched long and far in this connection, that if there is a workable incomes policy it has not yet been made clear—at any rate, an incomes policy in this sense of detailed regulation all round.

So I am forced to the conclusion, unpalatable to some on the cross-benches, I fancy, that the main instruments of control must be overall rather than particular. I am not a bit doctrinaire about this; I am equally prepared in theory to operate both with fiscal and with monetary policy. The essential desideratum in a situation in which the growth of spending is so much outstripping the growth of production is that, somehow or other, the stream of expenditure (the 'cash flow', if you like to expand Lord Thorneycroft's term) impinging on the stream of goods and services must not exceed the value of the latter at constant or, at worst, very slowly rising prices. If it is exceeding it, as it unquestionably is to-day, then the excess must cease.

Is this deflation? I can almost feel some noble Lords responding with this comment. Well, perhaps it is all a semantic question; but in my vocabulary, at least, 'deflation' means a reduction of spending power below the point at which it will sustain constant prices and incomes rising with productivity. What I am asking for is not that. I am not saying that the volume of spending power should not increase. I am saying that it should not increase faster, or much faster, than productivity. A noble Lord reminded us yesterday of Humpty Dumpty's saying that you can use words to make them mean what you want. But I seriously suggest that it is not helpful to the understanding of what is really involved in this deeply serious situation in which we find ourselves if you call what is in fact a reduction of an excess rate of increase by the same term as you would apply to the creation of a positive deficiency.

The implication of this policy is simple enough and, I should have thought it to be—and I hope that I have said enough already to convince noble Lords that my sympathies are in some respects neither with the giants on one side or the pygmies on the other, to use one noble Lord's interesting terminology—eminently reasonable. Indeed, I would say that it is an incomes policy, but it is an incomes policy without the immense practical difficulties and political frictions inevitably associated with such a policy as usually propounded.

[At this point an inquiry was put by Lord Brown: was I implying that by the restriction of money supply you can stop the powerful unions from extracting large wage increases?]

My Lords, I am coming to that; I am not going to dodge the question. This is an incomes policy which, while containing aggregate demand within appropriate limits, leaves initiative as regards particular rates to the parties immediately concerned. On this view the Government should say to business and to the trade unions, 'We do not in the least go back on the policy, supported by all parties since the Coalition White Paper, of avoiding deflation, of endeavouring to secure, through fiscal and monetary policy, a volume of demand which, rising with production, will sustain adequate levels of employment. But beyond that we will not go, because to go beyond that involves debasing the standard; involves continued depreciation of money: and no group in the community, industrialists or workers, has the constitutional or moral right to demand that.'

The Government should go on to say, 'If any of you want that, it is your choice. You can have higher rates, but you must not expect the finance to be made available to provide a full use of labour and resources at that depreciating level of the value of money. We are not going to bail you out if you make bargains involving an excessive strain on the price level. Our policy is to maintain the purchasing power of money and a volume of demand which will provide high employment and incomes rising with productivity; just that.' My Lords, is that unreasonable? I ask, is it really true that the great trade unions, the hitherto soberly led trade unions, which have meant so much to the social life of this country, wish to make demands on the products of industry under which full employment can be maintained only by continuing inflation? I refuse to believe it.

That, my Lords, is a general statement. What should be done to translate it into practice? I am quite clear that we have to accept bygones as bygones. There can be no question of undoing the bargains that have been made in the last few months. Positive deflation, I say again, is no proper counter-measure to an inflation of the order of magnitude which has now occurred. The best we can hope for is to see that it does not go on; to contain what has happened; to prevent its continuing and to hope that, eventually, no further devaluation is implied. We cannot be certain of that. The rises of the last few months will take time—probably six months—to seep through; and although there is some inflation elsewhere, it is not nearly at the same rate in relation to productivity. The balance of payments, thank heaven, is favourable enough now, but it will not continue so for long if the inflation continues. Given this objective, let me make it perfectly clear that I have no doctrinaire objection to the use of the fiscal weapon.

Now, my Lords, I am going to say something that will shock my friends on the Government benches very much: that I personally should have been much happier if the Government had not promised to give away their savings until the crisis had passed. I certainly should not object, even now, to laying additional increases of purchase tax—on luxuries, for instance—where that is practicable. But in the circumstances I am afraid that much reliance will have to be placed on monetary policy; and, having regard to the effect on interest rates and investments, perhaps more than otherwise might be wished.

I am equally clear that the present mild measures are not yet enough. I have great sympathy for the Bank, and its very distinguished Governor, in this situation. Public opinion, and often the Bank's political masters, expect it to provide at once support for the gilt-edged market and a limitation on the provision for aggregate expenditure. But, of course, my Lords, in present circumstances the two objectives are not necessarily compatible. Unless, therefore, we are extraordinarily lucky—and I hope that we shall be—we must expect liquidity to become tighter and interest rates to become higher if the depreciation of the pound is to be arrested. And if we are disposed to grumble at that, do let us remember that, with the present rate of inflation, real rates of interest are not all that high. Suppose, my Lords, that prices are rising at the rate of 8 per cent *per annum*. A man who lends money to the government at that rate is in fact, poor fool! getting a zero return on his investment; and the government, or the borrower, is getting off very lightly indeed.

9 Collapse of Balance-of-Payments Surplus Predicted

Motion: Wilberforce Report and the Economic Situation; 3 March 1971

My Lords, it seems to me that there can be considerable debate among serious-minded people about the quantitative implications of the recommendations of the Committee of the noble and learned Lord, Lord Wilberforce. Are we to take the 10·9 per cent, which has been quoted in Government circles, as a proper measure of the increase, or are we to assume, as has been assumed from time to time in the discussion this afternoon, that it was a substantially higher figure? Personally, I am inclined to the latter view. I find it difficult to believe that the so-called lead-in productivity incentives are to be ignored when we are trying to estimate the net effect on aggregate expenditure in relation to output of what was recommended. I therefore tend to think (and I regret to say it) that the award in fact somewhat increases inflationary pressures.

But be that as it may, the salient fact of the situation is that even if the lowest figure be taken as authentic, the probable effect is still inflationary. The annual rate of growth in the economy at this time is not more than 3 per cent per annum. A rate of increase of incomes, even if restricted to the Government's target of 8 per cent, would still exceed this rate of growth by 5 per cent; and of course we know that in fact earnings in general are rising by much more than 8 per cent per annum. It is therefore surely no accident that prices are rising at a rate probably exceeding 8 per cent per annum. The *Economist* last week hazarded a guess that they would soon be rising at 10 per cent, and I see nothing in the situation which suggests that that conjecture is unwarranted.

This is a very grave situation. It is graver, I believe, than anything with which we have been confronted in the last 25 years. If we project this rate of inflation for another five or six years, our money will have lost a third of its purchasing power. If it goes on for ten years it will have lost half its purchasing power. I will not expatiate on what this implies to those of us who live on fixed incomes. There must be some, even in your Lordships' House, who are wondering whether their present expectation of life will expire before they are reduced to the lowest level of State-supported indigence. But I will emphasise the effect on culture. There can be no university, no institution for the purveyance of the higher branches of art or music, or drama, whose way of life, whose plan, whose very existence, is not threatened by such a development.

Nor should one neglect the effect of inflation in industry and production. In the demand-inflations of the past, profits tended to flourish, at any rate for a time. In the end liquidity complications usually set in because of deceptive accountancy and the catching up of public expectations with what was happening behind the public's back. But for the time being, if you have a demand inflation, there may be positively beneficial effects upon investment. But in cost-inflations profits are squeezed from the outset, and we see already to-day the effects on investment of declining profit margins. If this goes on, let there be no doubt that the rate of growth, far from increasing, will be even slower than it is to-day.

I would add—although in the last analysis I should regard this as a secondary matter—that since I do not believe that the rest of the world will go on to inflate as rapidly as we are inflating at the moment, I do not believe that we shall be able to hold the much vaunted surplus in the balance of payments very long. If the present inflation goes on, the surplus in the balance of payments will be gone like the snows of this afternoon. There is nothing but trouble ahead even if the rate of increase in incomes is kept down to the Government's present target figure.

What are we to do about this? It is inconceivable that any government in this country should allow such a situation to continue. Despite all our mistakes, made, if I may say so, by all governments since the war; despite our unwillingness, widespread among the public, to face facts, we have not yet acquired Latin-American habits. Men of good will of all parties want to break out of the vicious circle. The question is, how? There are some, I know, some whom I greatly respect, who place their hopes on an increase in production. But I am afraid this is self-deception. Of course an increase of growth, other things being equal, would help.

Supposing that the gap between the rate of inflation and the present rate of increase of earnings were (shall we say?) 1 or 2 per cent, I would not say that we could not hope for salvation this way. But we must have a quantitative perspective here. The gap is not of that order. The gap is much more likely to be the difference between 3 per cent and 13 per cent. I ask seriously, does anyone in his senses believe that the gap can be quickly closed in that way? The most that we have achieved in recent years in the way of an annual growth rate has been between 5 and 6 per cent, which is not more than half-way in the right direction. And remember that these accelerations, taking place in periods of what might be called ultra-full employment, did not last.

Moreover, I would say—and I say it with regret, knowing that what I am saying will be antipathetic to many whom I admire and respect on the

Opposition and the Liberal benches—that I think there is a real danger that in seeking to stimulate growth by indiscriminate financial measures, the net effect might easily be to increase the gap between aggregate demand and production and so to move to a further increase in the rate of inflation. I am not against growth—heaven forbid!—but in the present circumstances I urge your Lordships to realise that with the inflationary gap of the size that it is at the moment, to rely upon growth as the main cure is to rely on wishful thinking.

My Lords, it is surely equally clear—or should be equally clear—that this is not a problem to be solved by widespread changes in the industrial structure. In my young days, when I thought of myself as a revolutionary socialist—a very mild and inoffensive one, I can assure your Lordships— we used to say that if only one nationalised the means of production, distribution and exchange, all would be well and the problem of industrial relations would be solved. Well, my Lords, we have not gone the whole hog, but we have nationalised a good deal, and I have not noticed that the pressure for wage increases higher than the rate of growth has noticeably diminished in those areas. I would not wish to extenuate employers in the private sector for concessions on a similar scale, but I do submit that the fact that the employer is the public rather than private enterprise is no safeguard against cost inflation, to put it very mildly.

Furthermore, I would add that quantitatively it is equally clear that if all profits were abolished to-morrow, or appropriated for the payment of other incomes, it would not meet claims of the order we are now encountering without a continuous rise of prices. According to the Treasury White Paper, the trading profits of companies in the last year for which we have records, after providing for stock appreciation and capital consumption, were only 8·8 per cent of total domestic production. You cannot meet wage claims, or income claims of any kind, of the sort which are coming forward now without rising prices. The fundamental problem is that if prices are assumed to be constant, then the current level of claims is asking for more from the machine than the machine will turn out, and consequently prices rise.

So, my Lords, the real dilemma of the situation is this: that given the present rate of growth, or the present conceivable increase of growth in the short period, if the demand for increased earnings adds up to more than this rate, then inescapably one of two things follows: either finance is produced to meet the demand, in which case prices rise, or it is not, in which case, lamentably, unemployment increases. That is the situation, as I see things, in which we find ourselves at present, and it is not easy to find a way out. The value of money is being lowered month by month by demands on the product of industry which it is impossible to meet at constant prices. And this is, surely, not a position which any British Government can afford to acquiesce in for long.

Now may I say at once that I do not believe that the policy of cutting off immediately, either by monetary or by fiscal means, all sources of finance for the upward movement is either practical or prudent. So violent an application of the financial brakes as that would indeed bring widespread bankruptcy and unemployment, involving all sorts of enterprises which at present regard themselves as moderately stable. And remember, my Lords, that the application of the financial brakes to a rate of increase of aggregate expenditure not exceeding the rate of growth of the economy is not deflation. Deflation, surely, in any intelligible sense of the word, is a contraction of expenditure below the current rate of production so that prices fall or unemployment increases. To restrict the rate of expenditure to an annual increase corresponding to the rate of growth is not deflation. It is indeed the norm of monetary stability which should be the long period objective of us all. But, my Lords, I agree that to put on the brakes as violently as that in the short period would be neither practical nor prudent. So, in principle, I agree with the aim of decelerating the upward financial movement rather than bringing it at once to a full stop by monetary or fiscal means.

But, my Lords, this does not mean that I see the same reason for accepting claims of the present order of magnitude in the market for services. Any grounds for accepting anything beyond the average rate of growth in this connection must be justified by quite different con-siderations, considerations of relativities in closely connected industries, delayed adjustments in the past, or, as in the obvious case of the police force, exceptional difficulties of recruitment. And I am bound to say that in my opinion even 10·9 per cent for electricity workers or 9 per cent for postmen leaves me with little hope of seeing the rate of inflation reduced in the near future.

Let us be clear about one thing, even though it may not be an immediate guide to policy. If the average rate of claim for increased earnings were no greater than the increased rate of growth, then the solution of this frightful problem would be in sight. There would indeed be a pretty considerable backlog of illiquidity and increased costs to be worked off; but, given the assurance of that degree of realism, I am pretty confident that these difficulties could be surmounted. But how are we to get to such a position? At the moment, the policy seems to be to resist, or to appear to resist, demands which are higher than the still highly inflationary 8 to 12 per cent level, to resist these in the public sector, to deprecate them in the private sector, and to maintain something of a credit squeeze. I cannot say that I think that this is very drastic; and I have said already once before in your Lordships' House that I do not think it is made psychologically more commendable to the workers by concessions at this stage in income tax, much as I believe tax reform to be long overdue.

I suppose that this policy has some chance of succeeding. One of the senior economists in this country, one who has been right more times than most others about the way in which the economy has been tending from time to time, said to me only the other day that he thought it had a 25 per cent chance of succeeding. I personally should put it rather higher than that. But of this I feel convinced: if it does not show some signs of succeeding within the next few months—and by success I mean, let me reiterate, incomes rising not greatly more than the current rate of economic growth—if it does not succeed in that sense, then I am inclined to think that some sort of freeze, some sort of incomes policy, will have to be attempted. I say this with very great regret and without very much hope. I am no more convinced than I ever have been that, in the long run, such policies are viable without the loss of many liberties to which the majority of us—and, I venture to say, the majority of trade unionists—attach great importance, or without the growth of evasions and corrupt practices which we should surely deplore.

I have listened with very great interest to what was said by the noble Baroness, Lady Wootton of Abinger, but I remain unconvinced. I have yet to hear of any variant of incomes policy which stands up to criticisms based either on the experience of such policies in the past or on the general common sense of the subject. A most remarkable article by two young men from the London School of Economics was published in the *Financial Times*, I think about three weeks ago, which I should have thought put paid to any hope of easy success in this direction. Yet I do not think this community can stand a rate of inflation of 8 to 10 per cent per annum for long. And if it goes on, then I am clear that we shall have to take some very blunt instruments to deal with it, to provide at least a period in which we may pause and think, and reshape our policies.

But how much better it would be if all concerned were to come to their senses and to realise that the sort of demands which are now being made on the product of industry are impossible of fulfilment without the consequences of either increased prices or increased unemployment! It is here that I cannot help feeling that the performance of the present Government, with all its courage and good intentions with which I sympathise, has fallen considerably short of what might have been wished. The present Government, believe me, have not succeeded in driving home to ordinary people the contradictions of the present position.

In this respect, my Lords, I submit that the public at large are in a state of split personality. They condemn rising prices, but they also condemn the means of stopping them. They deplore the erosion of the power to purchase of the money in their pockets, but they still contemplate with apparent equanimity claims or recommendations for pay increases which make such erosion inevitable. I ask: is it beyond the powers of reason and persuasion to resolve this schizoid condition? Is it asking too much of those who rule over us and at whose mercy we are, is it asking too much of men of good will in all parties, that they should try to get this fact over to the public? I do not know. But I do know that if this is not got over, then we are in for a very bad time indeed.

10 Inflation and Unemployment

Debate on the Address (concluded); 9 November 1971

My Lords, doubtless we can all agree that the centre of gravity of this discussion this afternoon is the level of unemployment. However, I would submit that near the centre of gravity is also the problem of the value of money still falling, prices still rising—even though less rapidly—at what at any other time in our political history would have been regarded as a deplorable rate.

I wonder whether it is sufficiently realised in this connection that we are faced with a problem which has not, to my knowledge, confronted any government in this country at any previous time in our history? Rising prices and rising unemployment are an extremely unusual combination. Usually, falling unemployment goes with rising prices. Usually, falling prices produce unemployment. But here, apparently, the reverse is the case. This, I suggest, should induce in noble Lords on the Opposition benches some degree of charity in considering the problems with which they and the present Government have been confronted. For I venture to submit that these two evils—unemployment and the disturbing decline in the value of money—are not altogether unconnected. This is not a mere coincidence of misfortune; in my submission, there is some connection between what has been happening. If your Lordships will bear with what to some of you may well seem to be a rather bleak and austere spelling out of the reasons why, I should like to dwell a little on this point.

The debate to-day has been more on party lines than earlier debates on the gracious Speech, but to my way of thinking the subject of debate to-day is not in the last analysis a party subject. It is essentially an intellectual problem, and I suggest that any solution thereof will present difficulties to either party. Let us suppose, for a moment, conditions rather more ideal than we are likely to see in the next few months or perhaps in the next few years. Let us suppose, for a moment, that there has been a period of stable prices and of incomes rising not more than the general rise in productivity. Clearly, we are a thousand miles away from that, but I ask your Lordships to forgive me, for the moment, if I dwell on such a situation. I think the contrast between that and the situation with which we are confronted to-day is instructive.

46

In such circumstances, if you had a stable price level and the level of incomes had not been rising more than productivity, and if unemployment at such a time were greater than what could be considered to be the irresistible norm due to change and friction and so on, then I should certainly say that the government of the day were severely to blame. I can conceive that years ago, if there were unemployment in such circumstances, it might have been argued that for some reason or other incomes were still too high. But that is a point of view which I think has been generally abandoned. At the present day, surely we should ask in those circumstances, 'Why put the burden of adjustment on incomes? Why not attack the cause of unemployment at its source?' And we should know what to do, for this is the paradox of the last 40 years of history. In the intervening period, I remember we used to say, 'Well, we all know how to deal with inflation, but the problem of dealing with deflation is much more difficult and it escapes us.' I have certainly said this in the past; but nothing could have been more completely wrong. The fact is that we do know how to deal with unemployment due to deflation, in the sense of falling prices: you simply ladle out purchasing power until the situation turns round. Our failure since the War in the sphere of macro-economics has not been in regard to deflation; it has been in regard to inflation.

Let me now come a little nearer to reality. Let us suppose, just for the sake of argument, that you have a situation in which prices are rising—that is to say, where the value of money is falling—at about 8 per cent per annum, which is not at all a satisfactory position. Just think, my Lords, of the position of all cultural institutions in such circumstances. Just think of the position of those living on pensions which are adjusted only at longish periods. At the same time, the incomes of those employed—wage earners, salary earners and so on—are rising more than that, at 12 per cent What happens? I shall not talk about what will happen to the balance of payments, because that depends so much on the rate of exchange and what is happening elsewhere; and you get into trouble with the balance of payments only if other people are not inflating as fast as you are. That is a danger which is not absolutely negligible, but it is not one upon which I wish to expatiate this afternoon.

But what will happen to employment in the circumstances that I have mentioned? What will be the effect on unemployment if the incomes of those employed are rising faster than the rise in prices? I confess that, on general grounds, I should expect more unemployment to occur. Outside comparatively narrow limits, I should not expect the difference to be made good out of profit margins. I should first expect business to try to redress the situation by raising prices to keep up with the rise in costs. Then, if there were restraints, if there were exhortations, if there were agreements to keep prices from rising so rapidly, I should expect business to react by trying to keep costs down by reducing the scale of their operations. And that, I suspect—to descend down to earth to what I believe to be reality; I may be wrong—is one of the things which has been happening to this country lately. Undoubtedly, prices have been rising, and undoubtedly the rise in prices has been due to inflation of some sort or another.

I listened last Thursday to a notable speech by the noble Lord, Lord Garnsworthy, on the rocketing of prices in the market for houses. It was a splendid speech, inspired by true humanitarian feelings, and the examples that he gave of hardship were such as to touch the hearts of all but the most stony-hearted. But the noble Lord seemed to think that this phenomenon of the housing market was a sort of spontaneous evil; something which was perhaps due to the machinations of a few evil-minded men, or something which had just hit us out of the blue. But the fact, surely, is that what is happening in the market for real estate is what always has happened throughout history when you have had an absence of confidence in the future value of money. I have no doubt at all, my Lords, that the rise in prices recently has been the result mainly of inflation, and I equally have no doubt that the proximate cause of the inflation has been the rise of costs. No one can deny—and I am not saying this in any tone of reproach at all—I am trying to be as objective as I can—that the wage settlements of recent years have involved rises more than any corresponding rise in productivity.

Now, my Lords, who is to blame? I personally do not feel disposed to make accusations. In my judgment, what we need at this critical juncture in our economic history is more understanding rather than more recriminations. But I am bound to say in all candour to my noble friends on the Opposition benches that I cannot understand the attitude of those who say that this Government, and this Government only, are wholly to blame. Surely what we are suffering from is a problem which began before that; a problem which began under the last Government. The noble Lord, Lord Delacourt-Smith, in a speech of beautiful lucidity and moderation of tone, almost seemed to suggest at one stage of his speech that in 1970 the outgoing Government handed to the incoming Government a situation which was extremely easy to handle, and that if they had been sufficiently endowed with wisdom, which no doubt would have been forthcoming from his side of the House, everything would have been lovely. I find it extraordinarily difficult to believe that, great as is my respect for the intellect concentrated on the Opposition front bench, and indeed behind it.

I would say, not making recriminations, that what we are suffering from, both by way of unemployment and by way of the decline in the value of money, can be described in less personal terms, in more objective terms: the results, if you like, of the present institutional structure in the labour market; the by-product of certain habits which have developed in collective bargaining; the by-product of an increase in the volume of credit more than what was ideally desirable in the circumstances; the result of wage settlements by arbitrators taking too much notice of minute problems of relativity and too little notice of the effects of the settlements that they awarded on the economy as a whole. I would say that what we are suffering from at the moment in the last analysis, and what is intractable for the present Government—and what would be intractable for Her Majesty's Opposition if they were to come into power—is the general state of bewilderment among the public generally; the general state of bewilderment among people of good will concerning what is happening to us and the relationship between prices, incomes and employment, and so on and so forth.

Now, my Lords, what is to be done about all this? I think I know the solution of the stabilisation problem which would be most congenial to me in tranquil and ideal conditions. I formulate the ideal stabilisation policy as one which involves a control by the Government of aggregate expenditures such as to keep the value of money constant with reasonably full employment and wages and other incomes rising not faster than productivity. Whether this is done by financial means or whether it is done by fiscal means is to me a secondary matter. I am eclectic about this; I am open to argument about it. One can talk about it a great deal, but that is a technical matter. The norm seems to me to be a reasonable one: that the aggregate expenditure should not be such as to bring about inflation, but shuld be such as to permit a rise in the level of incomes, especially wages, equal to productivity or, if you are willing to put up with a little inflation, not more than $1\frac{1}{2}$ or 2 per cent more than that. If that policy were adopted in normal and tranquil conditions, I would say that what happened after that would be up to the employers and the trade unions, and if they chose to exceed that norm then they would be answerable for the consequences.

We are miles away from normal conditions, and the application of that particular prescription assumes starting from an even level, a level where unemployment is in some sense or other normal, however you may define that. And, lamentably, that is not our position at all. Our position at the present time, despite the reassuring remarks of the noble Lord speaking from the Government benches earlier, is still one of continuing inflation, slowing down perhaps, but still inflation; and at the same time the volume of unemployment now is such as to mean a most substantial waste of productive resources, not to mention human anxiety and suffering. In such circumstances, I would freely admit that to put the brakes on so as to secure immediately a slowing down of the rate of aggregate expenditure in order to match exactly the rise in productivity would certainly intensify depression and unemployment. I suggest that no responsible person would advocate so sudden an application of the brakes as all that.

Our problem is rather the problem of slowing down the rise of prices and at the same time of increasing the volume of employment. It is clear (is it not?) that if incomes were to cease to rise more than productivity this problem would be nearly solved. I will not say that it would be entirely solved because there are deep problems of regional unemployment (on which the noble Lord, Lord Delacourt-Smith, spoke so eloquently) which would not be solved directly by these aggregate measures; but I think that the noble Lord, Lord Drumalbyn, was right when he said that if you have a buoyant economy, the regional problems are *ipso facto* easier to solve. I am quite sure that if the rise of incomes were more related to the rise of productivity, the whole situation would become more manageable. Then concessions on the part of the Chancellor in regard to taxation, innovations in government expenditure and so on, designed to relieve unemployment, could be carried out without the lurking fear that the inflation will persist. I do not believe that in those circumstances the rise in incomes would be zero; on the contrary, I am inclined to think that in recent months productivity per head has risen so considerably that the economy could look forward to a level of productivity per head larger than in recent years and consequently capable of sustaining without inflation a more sub-stantial rise of wages without producing unemployment.

It is considerations of that sort which lead to the search for an incomes policy on the part of so many men of good will. I have said in this House before, and I should like to say it again, that much as I have disagreed with many of those who have advocated an incomes policy, and sceptical as I remain of the availability of a cut-and-dried solution in this connection, I honour those—and especially those on the Opposition benches—who, running the risk of incurring unpopularity among their own fellows, have insisted on the point that I am trying to make. If there were available some incomes policy, some method of disciplining the rise in incomes so that aggregate expenditure can be let out without giving rise to inflation and perhaps to unemployment, we should all surely be able to go home much happier. I say that I respect this point of view; but I must confess that I am still a little sceptical about such expedients as long-term policies. I see tremendous difficulties in the control of wage relativities from year to year from any central authority. I see great possibilities of cumulative evasion. I think that both employers and employed would know all sorts of ways round it. I confess that in the long run, once the present difficulties were over, I would prefer to trust to macro-economic control of aggregate expenditure and a greater public understanding of the issues involved than at present exists. But, certainly in present circumstances, I would not rule out on principle any expedient which would stop the inflation and help employment.

Lord Rhodes asked whether I would include price control in 'not ruling out' any expedient. I am much more sceptical of the efficiency of price control in solving the unemployment problem than I should be of the efficacy of incomes control; because price control by squeezing still further the profit margins might easily induce individual corporations, whether private or public, to seek to economise still further on manpower. If the noble Lord can show me cases of monopolistic price extortions which need to be controlled he will not find me doctrinaire in refusing to accept.

I say that I do not see an easy way by the traditional methods. The control of prices and incomes under the Labour Government was not stupendously successful. If it were re-imposed I think it might work for a time, but I should fear that after a time it would break down and that there might be pent up behind this temporary stoppage demands greater than they might have been in the absence of it. But I am not sure. If the Government were to introduce that sort of measure as an emergency in one of the unforeseen contingencies which may arise in this difficult situation with which we are faced, I am not sure that I should do very much eyebrow-raising at that stage.

Let me turn to other ideas which are prevalent and which are also open to some objection. I read with great interest the other day the Wincott Lecture by my great friend Professor James Meade in which, arguing with his accustomed persuasiveness and lucidity, he recommended that there should be a suspension of certain privileges regarding Supplementary Benefits and so on in the event of strikes which are due to unagreed claims exceeding certain norms laid down by the Government. One must treat with great respect the point of view of a man who, behind the scenes, certainly did more than anyone except Maynard Keynes in inducing the Coalition Government to accept the present pledges with regard to employment policies. But, having said that, I must say that I see great and obvious difficulties, loopholes, in Professor Meade's suggestions. What if employers and employed agreed to exceed his stated norms? Then none of his sanctions come into operation and we are off again. Personally, I have played about with the idea of some sort of tax on employers who make agreements exceeding norms of a certain average income per head, but I find it difficult to believe that it would be politically acceptable. There are also some quite formidable administrative difficulties, although I do not think that they would be insurmountable. In any case, I would think of such a thing only as an emergency measure; in the long run it would be possible to shoot holes through it with a very inaccurate gun.

Thus, my Lords, I confess that I must end on a sober note. I find it very hard to take as optimistic a view of the present position as did the noble Lord, Lord Drumalbyn, and other members of the Government. Certainly I think that the measures which the Chancellor of the Exchequer and the Government have taken could produce—and I stress 'could produce'—some upturn, provided that confidence is restored; provided that there exists a confidence that the future is going to be better, that inflationary wage claims are not going further to deplete cash flows and diminish incentives to investment. But that restoration of confidence depends on a state of affairs on all sides which has yet to be established. It is difficult to be sanguine that people at large are yet persuaded of the necessary relationships between prices, incomes, production, and so on, which must obtain if our way is to be smooth both in regard to employment and also in regard to the value of money. I say, therefore, that a heavy responsibility rests upon all concerned; upon Government and Opposition; upon both parties to collective bargaining and to those responsible for the formation of public opinion in regard to these vitally important matters.

11 The Floating Pound and the Corrupting Influence of Inflation

Motion: The Economic Situation, Inflation and Unemployment; 5 July 1972

My Lords, I rise to make a speech about inflation, but I do so with considerable trepidation, having regard to the speeches which have preceded mine. I should conceive myself to be, so to speak, between Scylla and Charybdis. I must be careful not to incur the reproach of my colleague, the noble Baroness, Lady Seear, for being a prophet of doom. Of course, I would agree with her that a prospective rate of increase in the level of retail prices of between 8 and 10 per cent per annum, as has been predicted in certain quarters, is not the same as the rate of increase during the hyper-inflation on Continental Europe immediately after the War, but I submit that it is something to be seriously alarmed about. On the other hand, much as I sympathise with the noble Earl who has just been defending the policy of the Government with much the same determination and ingenuity as his opponent the noble Lord, Lord Beswick, I seem to remember, defended his Government in rather similar circumstances when he was sitting where the noble Earl is sitting to-day, I refuse so far in the debate to be persuaded by the contention that, although there is certainly something to be a little worried about, there are all sorts of small signs which show that here and there is some statistical improvement and there is nothing more serious than what has been suggested in the last two speeches to worry about here and now.

May I begin with a comment on the events of last Friday week—the floating of the pound and the fall in the rate of sterling which has followed since that decision. I do not think that the present position in that respect affords any ground whatever for complacency. I believe that what has happened places us and our associates in the Free World in a position of greater danger than we were in before last Friday week. If I turn first to the domestic situation, I would say that what has happened so far—perhaps it may be reversed—will certainly, as I think the noble Lord, Lord Beswick, said, have some influence on the cost of living; and if it has some influence on the cost of living it then makes Her Majesty's Government's task in

53

controlling cost inflation greater than would otherwise have been the case. Secondly, I would submit that what happened is likely to introduce—I choose my words carefully at this point—complications in our progress towards our entry into Europe and participation in progressive policies therein.

I agree with the remark which has been made by several commentators that a float at some stage might well have proved to be necessary; and, to the extent that the step has now been taken, there is some local easement so far as our competitive position is concerned. But one must remember that what is our easement is other people's disadvantage. I do not think that it took the remarks attributed to M. Pompidou only yesterday, or the day before, to convince many of us that if the float continues downwards difficulties of all kinds hitherto unsuspected are likely to confront Her Majesty's Government in their onward progress. Certainly I would say that what happened last Friday week was some menace to the financial stability of the Free World in general.

The noble Earl referred to the desirability of international monetary reconstruction, but for obvious reasons of time he did not reveal at all precisely the thoughts that were passing through his head. It is my submission that a change in the rate of sterling, to put it mildly, is not making it easier for the position of the dollar, and if the position of the dollar is still further weakened, then even the much praised—not by me— Smithsonian agreement (I never thought it would last) will be considerably weakened. But, my Lords, having delivered myself of these fears, let me say at once that I believe the decision was a right one. If I had been, as I once was, a public servant, advising Ministers, I should have given the same advice in the circumstances.

But, having said that, I must say— someone must say it—that some, at least, of the explanations and the extenuations which have been given seem to me to be unadulterated nonsense. To me it is almost inconceivable how intelligent and upright and straightforward men can still go on invoking the time-honoured reproaches against speculators. I ask you, my Lords, to reflect upon the impact on humble men and women of the world not involved in the political badminton, so to speak, when they hear once again in a currency crisis this sort of accusation. It only needs a member of the Government to get up and say that 'The pound in your pocket will still purchase the same amount' for one to be able to say, 'Well, this is where I came in before'.

The reason for the pickle that we are in and the figure that we cut in the outside world is not the gnomes of Zurich, not just bad luck, not the wickedness of real estate proprietors, not even our failure to grow at a faster rate, although of course a faster rate of growth would ease the situation. We deceive ourselves if we think that any conceivable rate of growth achievable within the next two years would eliminate the inflationary danger. No, my Lords, the villain of the piece is clearly in the dock; the villain of the piece is inflation—and our inflation. Since 1962 retail prices in this country have risen over 60 per cent, and certainly the blame for that is not to be attributed uniquely to either of the parties which have held the reins of power during that period. Surely we should all agree that whenever the inhabitants of one area are subjected to an inflation greater than that which is going on elsewhere—and that, on the whole, is what has been happening here; there are one or two others which surpass us in the table, but not many—then inevitably pressure on the exchanges develops; and if people expect inflation, as they certainly have expected inflation and as they had every right to expect it, as the events have proved, then if they have the facilities, they take steps to remove their funds to safer quarters. If the inflation goes on, their prudence is justified by the security of money and possibly by a spot of capital gain.

Let us forget the external situation for a moment. Let us forget all about the outside world and be as insular as we like to be these days. In passing, I must say that I view with the greatest apprehension the disposition in certain quarters (not, I am sure, on this front bench) to say, 'Now the rate is floating the balance of payments will take care of itself'. The rate will continue to float downwards if the inflation goes on, and that is all that can be said about that one.

We cannot discuss everything at once. The Motion before us deals generally with internal matters, and it is to these internal matters that I should like to direct your Lordships' attention. Why should we bother about inflation? Why should we be alarmed at whatever rate has prevailed in the last 12 months and the rate which has been predicted by the National Institute of Economic Research (with which I happen for once to agree) for the next months ahead? I will not detain your Lordships by dwelling on the misery, the anxiety, caused to people on fixed private incomes, although anyone who has friends and relative in that position will well know all that it involves. But, after all, they are the weaker members of the community; perhaps they are in a minority; certainly if the trade unions continue to be strong, if profits go up, the votes of those weaker members of the community do not matter all that much. I will not dwell on that. I would rather dwell on something even deeper. I would say to your Lordships that inflation as we have known it through history—inflation even at this rate—corrupts and distorts the whole basis of the society in which we live.

My Lords, let me reassure the noble Baroness: I do not say that the world will come to an end if we degenerate to the position of Latin America. I agree with her that we are not that way yet, although we are some way towards it. After all, Latin America survives, after its fashion. What I do say is that inflation of the order of magnitude that we are contemplating gradually brings about a radical change in outlook, a change in outlook throughout society generally, which I personally regard as quite deplorable.

Let me give your Lordships a few examples. To keep in step with the noble Baroness, let me start with Latin America. Some years ago I paid a visit to a delightful country in that continent. My wife and I had the good fortune to be met at the boat by an ex-pupil, who conducted us with amazing celerity through the Customs. Having been brought up in the atmosphere of our stable society and in a Puritan household I was certainly extremely shocked when friends told me, 'Had you not been accompanied by a Government official you would not have got through those Customs for a week unless you had been prepared to pay a bribe'. I say, my Lords, that I was shocked at that. But when I learned that those officials had their salaries revised only once a year and inflation at that time was proceeding at the brisk pace of about 5 per cent per month, I began to realise that after all there was no reason to feel quite so superior. What should we do if we were in a similar position?

But now let us come nearer home and consider for a moment the purchase of property. Supposing a Member of your Lordships' House had been approached in the stable days by a young couple setting up house together. Surely a wise course would have been—and ancient instances would have been justifiably adduced—to counsel prudence against running into debt, prudence in over-optimistic anticipation of future income. 'Be careful, my boy,' you might have said, 'never run into debt if you can help it.' But, my Lords, supposing you were in that avuncular position to-day and you were considering the interests of the young couple, you would surely say to them, 'Borrow as much as you can and repay in depreciated currency'. Is that a happy state of affairs? Is that a state of affairs which is ultimately conducive to a stable moral society?

Let me take a further example which is, I suggest, to people of integrity, much more worrying than that, namely, the sale of National Savings Certificates. Let me take a simple figure. Supposing anyone had bought £100 worth of Savings Certificates in the middle of 1967. I choose my dates so as to be equally fair, so to speak, to both sides of the House in this respect. By now, at the rate that was quoted then, that £100 would have appreciated to £125. But in the same period retail prices have risen from 119 to 162 so that the real value of the original investment plus interest would now be just a little below £92; that is to say, this purchaser would have been lending money to the Government at a negative rather than a positive rate of interest.

Surely that is a disturbing thought. I say this with deadly earnestness. It is a disturbing thought that some of the least knowledgeable members of the community have been induced by some of the most patriotic and public-spirited to buy assets supposed to be increasing in value but actually diminishing. Now of course this fact is quite obvious to any one with any financial training whatever, but it is very seldom mentioned and I think I know why. I have often been asked myself to take a seat on a platform recommending the sale of National Savings Certificates and I have always refused. The reasons why I have refused are two-fold: in the first place I did not want to be an embarrassment to my colleagues on the platform, for whose good intentions I have the highest regard; in the second place I had the feeling, which is certainly justified by analysis, that if the will to save is undermined, and if instead of saving people rush into commodities, then the inflationary pressure is increased. All that is true. But I ask noble Lords in all parts of the House: do we really wish to save our bacon at the expense of the poor and the ignorant? If the Government want to encourage saving—and I submit that they should want to encourage it— then they must provide some assurance that savers will not suffer. In the end they must control the value of money.

What is the cause of all our troubles? To keep our heads in this matter, to establish a proper sense of proportion, let us always remember that the supply of money—the credit base, if you like—and therefore the maintenance of the value of money, is definitely a responsibility of Government. Wherever else a policy of *laisser faire* may be justified it can never be justified here. It is no good any government saying that the supply of money is something which adapts itself to the needs of trade. We have heard that one many times before. Indeed, I remember when I was a young man and at the time of the great German invasion, the then Governor of the Reichsbank made a public statement regretting that the many factories that he employed in printing paper money were not able to keep up with the needs of trade. No government can afford to adopt the attitude that money must be passive to the needs of trade. Galloping inflation eventually lies that way.

I would say, as a corollary of what I have said, that few things can be more certain than that if the increase of the credit base passes a certain figure—which of course has to be related to the rate of growth of the economy—then there will be inflation. Few things are more certain than that if the rate of increase of the supply of money is limited to the rate of increase of real production, it is unlikely—although not quite impossible— that prices will rise indefinitely. There is no need to be a dogmatic adherent of the quantity theory of money to believe that. Provided the increase of the credit base is restrained then the value of money is not likely to fall for very long at an alarming rate. But, as the noble Lord, Lord Beswick, has pointed out, the credit base in recent months has been increasing at 20 per cent per annum.

This is not the end of the matter. If we were in a state of pre-existing stable prices, if we continued the control of the money supply and combined it with prudence in public finance, then it is very improbable that the price level would rise very much. But if inflation is already in operation, if people's expectations are geared up to further rises in the cost of living, and if we are in a condition in which there come forward claims for rates of pay far beyond any conceivable increase in productivity, then if extra finance is not available there must be unemployment. I am speaking in very rough terms here. Of course you can conceive of small excess increases which only give rise to small unemployment or small inflation. In such circumstances there might even be a hope that some small increases in rates of pay of that sort might be made at the expense of profit after taxation. But certainly any claims for increases of the order of magnitude of recent years cannot be met in that way, by conceivable achievable rates of growth. A 10 per cent rate of increase of earnings per annum cannot be met save by some inflation; and claims such as, rightly or wrongly, have been reported in the Press in the last day or so for increases of a further 30 per cent, if generalised, must lead either to widespread unemployment or to rampant widespread inflation.

What then must we do? I am quite sure that if the Government regard the money supply as infinitely elastic, to be manipulated simply to be responsive passive to the needs of trade, and if interest rates are kept at what, having regard to the rate of inflation, is an artificially low level, any arrangements, however intelligent and well-conceived, will break down. I do not believe that the situation will be cured by mere exhortation, invocations of common solidarity and so on. We have had so much of that ever since the war that, so far as the ordinary man not involved in politics is concerned, it falls stale and unprofitable on deaf ears. Arbitration, special inquiries—well, we have seen the results of arbitration and special inquiries in the last few catastrophic months. Nor do I believe that if employers and employed are left to themselves, even in the most conciliatory mood, much restraint will necessarily follow. As in the case of arbitration proceedings, the disposition will be, especially if the credit base goes on enlarging, to split the difference and take out the rest in rising prices. If the discussions are sectional rather than simultaneous to all industries, then the discussions will almost certainly resolve themselves into acrimonious debates about relativities; and once you start debating relativities once more you are involved in the vicious circle.

Nevertheless, my Lords, having said all that, let me add, lest there be any misunderstanding, that I am quite clear that if the Government were suddenly to put on the brakes on national expenditure, either by way of measures of public finance or by greatly slowing down the rate of increase of money, the result would be, with expectations geared up as they are now to inflation, a colossal depression. I know no case in history where inflation of the order of magnitude of that from which we are now suffering has been stopped by measures of this sort without that sort of effect.

Hence, although direct control of incomes as a long-run policy is likely to break down, and does indeed carry with it many dangers to a free society, I am forced to the conclusion that in order to create a breathing space in which expectations can be revised and clear understandings reached, I hope between the two parties, on the desirable future financial policy, the Government will be forced to impose some sort of control. I say this without any great hope that it will be very efficient or very just, or that it will be a final solution. And I abstain from discussing possible variants, save that I would express what I have said before in this House, a certain *penchant* for the solution thrown out by the noble Baroness, which she called the Hungarian solution; namely, the fixing of norms and penalisation of employers if those norms are exceeded. What I am clear about is that if inflation is allowed to proceed at the present rate—and I am sorry to say that nothing the noble Earl the Leader of the House has said persuades me that there is not a great danger (I would simply put it that way) that it will continue at the present rate—then I fear that the very foundations of our free and liberal society will be severely shaken.

12 Reduction of the Rate of Inflation— Essential Desideratum

Counter-Inflation (Temporary Provisions) Bill Motion: Approval; 23 November 1972

My Lords, it is the tradition in this House that we should seek so far as possible to establish a consensus—that we should not only brings out points of difference but points of agreement. I take it that we are all convinced at the moment that the value of money has been diminishing, is still diminishing and that that diminution must be arrested, if not completely stopped. In this connection, I was surprised to hear the noble Lord, Lord Diamond, to whom I always listen with respect and interest, base his indictment in this context entirely on what has happened in the last two years. If one takes the retail price index for 1963 as 100, the price in August of this year was 165, and although I should be the last person to wish to defend what has been allowed by ministers in the last two years, I should have thought, speaking with the utmost friendliness and deference, that those who sit on the Opposition benches would feel no reason to be altogether proud of what happened while they were in control. After all, the tremendous increase in the rate of increase of money supply began before the last General Election.

These differences apart, I wish to comment a little further on the question of property prices and the price of land. In recent debates I have noticed a growing tendency on the Labour Benches for noble Lords to pick out extraordinary cases of vast increases, which no one in his senses would deny, and to suggest that these were not only indicative of something wrong in the economy, which again no one would deny, but also that they constituted as it were one of the main causes. I have no doubt that the spectacle of the rising prices of land and real property is a cause of irritation and disquiet and may contribute to the general atmosphere of mutual distrust which makes grown-up and amicable discussion of these matters very difficult. I have no doubt also that there may be elements in the tax system favourable to an increase of demand in certain parts of the market for real estate. But, in the main, I suggest that to diagnose the rising prices of real property, or indeed of durable goods in general, as being one of the origins of the recent acceleration of the decline in the value of money is an absolutely classic case of mistaking effects for causes.

There is, of course, a certain amount of speculation in the narrow sense of the word—professional people cleverly attuned to the tendencies of the market making a 'bob' or two now and then—but I would be so bold as to say that, viewing the economy as a whole, the effect of this speculation in the narrow sense is quite negligible when compared with the effect of the surge into goods caused by the expectation of still rising prices. The fact is that one cannot fool all the people all of the time. Although at the beginning of the post-war period the decline in the value of money was not so perceptible, except to people living on fixed incomes, as to cause serious alarm—one shrugged one's shoulders and said, 'It all comes out in the wash and a little of that does not do much harm'—people are now aware that something serious is happening. This inclines men's minds, be they rich or poor, to seek some more stable repository for whatever they have.

What the Government have been doing—perhaps I should not refer solely to the Government but should widen the indictment and say what those who rule over us have been doing—in the last decade is to turn most of us into 'bulls' in real things and 'bears' in money; and to indicate the results of this sort of market movement as being one of the causes of what is happening seems to be as futile as if, when sticking a thermometer into a bowl of boiling water, one says, 'What a wonderful heater it is!'

Let me give an example. I know a youngish couple who came into a very few thousand pounds only a month or two ago. What did they do? Did they buy Savings Certificates or Savings Bonds? No. Did they go to some sober stockbroker and ask for a selected bunch, even of equities, which would perhaps maintain the value of the money they had come into? No. At the weekend they got into a car with their young family and they sallied forth into a part of the country where they thought that land prices had not risen as much as elsewhere because they felt confident that there, at any rate, they would have something which, in default of a total social revolution, might have some chance of keeping its value. That is what I am saying. The general bearishness with regard to money that is driving us all into goods and land is simply the leading species of a large genus.

What then can I say regarding the causes of inflation? As the noble Lord, Lord Balogh, has said this is a very complicated matter indeed. Inflation can come on the demand side from increased spending by individuals or, what is much more likely, by governments. It can come, too, on the cost side as a result of demands for increased emoluments at a high or low level, such demands influencing costs and eventually influencing prices. In the last twenty years many influences have been operative and I am sure that, if we were to get down to details, those of us who, like the noble Lord, Lord Balogh, and myself, have devoted a good deal of time to studying these matters would still find ourselves in some state of disagreement about the interpretation of particular phases. There certainly was a time when Lord

Balogh was insisting—perhaps rightly—more on the cost-push element when I was insisting on the existence of forces on the demand side. That is still a matter for detailed investigation, and I know of only one book that I would recommend to your Lordships—and it is now many years out of date—which, to my way of thinking, represents a scientific investigation of the problem.*

But, my Lords—and this is the point I want to make—none of these influences could operate as they have operated unless there was undue elasticity of the credit base. Spending would not increase for long unless the money supply was increasing at a rate disproportionate to the increase in productivity. Firms could not put up prices effectively in order to meet increased costs unless there was plenty of money about; and that has been the state of affairs during the last few years. To explain the contemporary rates of inflation without mentioning that is to get one's explanation completely out of perspective. When I hear minute discussion of this and that social evil—and there is usually something wrong somewhere, even if it is only the weather—adduced as explanations of the main evil from which we are suffering on this side, without mentioning the increase in the credit base, I am reminded of the parable of the American who could see the fly on the barn door but could not see the barn door itself.

I suggest that what I am talking about now is something that is very serious. How increases in the money supply affect prices is clearly a matter of great difficulty, and one about which professional opinion is by no means united, even at the present day. But confronted with the vast increases of the last few years, these differences are nothing—they are dust in the balance. Since the last months of the Labour Government the increases of the credit base have been such that it would be a miracle if there were not inflation. Over 20 per cent, as the noble Lord, Lord Diamond reminded us, with present growth rates, is just a recipe for trouble; and when the noble Lord, Lord Balogh, the other day, in a question to the noble Earl, the Lord Privy Seal, pointed out the rate at which the present deficit is running (which may easily amount to £4,000 million, or something like that) it is very difficult to understand the frame of mind which questions it as a cause—or the frame of mind which continues to permit it. It is no exaggeration to say that at the present time present measures are not successful. We are in a position reminiscent of the beginning of the great Continental inflations of this century. To my way of thinking it is incredible that ministers are not more alarmed than they allow themselves to appear in public.

If that is so, my Lords—and I am putting this question dispassionately at the moment and not as necessarily representing my own view—is not the obvious cure to stop the excess increase, to decree forthwith that the rate of increase of money supply shall not be greater than the anticipations

---

* J. C. R. Dow, *Management of the British Economy 1945–60* (London, 1965).

of increased productivity; or, perhaps to allow just a little elbow room for such degree of secular inflation as may relax the grip of the rentier and not do a great deal of harm to anybody within the lifetime of any person who is now aged, let us say, 35. That rhetorical recommendation is of course the serious recommendation of some, the serious recommendation of the extreme monetarists, the sort of overtone which emerges when Mr Enoch Powell makes one of these monolithic pronouncements on the principles of economic liberalism, which, I will confess to your Lordships, usually make me want to stand on a chair and sing 'The Red Flag'. Alas! I do not think that things are as easy as the Powellite pronouncements would suggest. I do not deny—and I believe that in this I could carry the noble Lord, Lord Balogh, with me—that inflation might be stopped by violent measures of this sort; but much else would be stopped as well.

These are controversial matters, but, speaking personally, I have no doubt at all that, with so many expectations in the economy geared up to continuing inflation at rates which have been prevalent in recent years, to put on the brakes as suddenly as that, with no other accompanying measures, would precipitate unemployment and stagnation of a kind not witnessed since the war. I suggest that all economic history bears out that view. When has a great inflation been stopped by purely monetary measures without precipitating difficulties of that sort at the same time? This is, if you like, a middle-period judgment. In the end one might hope that the machine will start again. There is a great deal of ruin in a nation. But in the meantime, how much suffering, how much social division and how much chaos will be engendered! It is for that reason, my Lords, and not because I have very great enthusiasm, or indeed confidence, that I support the Bill now before your Lordships' House. I have no illusions about freezes. I have no illusions about more complicated measures operating directly on prices and incomes. Freezes tend to disintegrate; people find a way round. Orthodox prices and incomes measures tend to be ineffective in the long run. But in the situation in which we find ourselves now, these measures, I submit, are the main hope of a diminution of the rate of increase of money supply without an undue check to growth and employment. If nothing is done, either we get catastrophic depreciation or we get catastrophic unemployment. The justification for the measure which the noble Lord, Lord Drumalbyn, has laid before the House this afternoon, with all its possible imperfections, is that it affords a breathing space in which to think out better ways of procedure.

I will conclude with this point. I do not think that this policy is going to be at all easy. I have little hope myself that 90 days will be sufficient to devise measures which will lead us into the new Jerusalem, or even perhaps 150 days. The frame of mind of some people—some of them friends of mine—who believe that after this period of freeze it will be possible just to relax into a free-for-all, much as I should like to agree with them, unregenerate economical liberal though I may be, seems to me to be an entirely unreal one. There is too great a head of inflationary steam in the economy for us to get out of our troubles as quickly as that. So I personally am convinced that when the freeze comes to an end there will still need to be some measures of control for some time. I retain the view that in a more rational atmosphere control of aggregate expenditure *via* some combination of control of money and the Budget, such control being directed to maintaining the increase of aggregate expenditure more or less in line with the increase in anticipated productivity, is the ideal. But I doubt whether a state of affairs which would permit reliance alone on that kind of policy is likely to come quickly.

So what is to happen? I confess that at this stage I become very puzzled. I listened with great respect to the speeches which preceded mine. I agree in principle, needless to say, with the sentiment expressed by Lord Diamond, that we must create an atmosphere in which it is felt by a sufficient number of people that there is fairness and justice all round. But we are a very long way, even among ourselves, from agreeing on what degree of fairness and justice can be expected at this time in history in this imperfect world. Take, for instance, the proposal of the Prime Minister which was unacceptable in the negotiations, that there should be just a flat rate of increase so far as all incomes are concerned. I doubt very much whether a proposal of that sort, or a proposal perhaps permitting a slightly easier position for the higher incomes, would be immediately acceptable to, let us say, Mr Clive Jenkins. The fight for relativities is quite as strong a social force as the fight on the part of more disinterested people for fairness and justice. And in the main I must say I am inclined to agree with the noble Baroness, Lady Seear, that when it is a question of helping the lower paid (apart from the question of abolishing structural imperfections such as the abominable restrictions on women's employment, with which she knows I am heartily in favour of what she has in mind) the best way is through revision of taxation rather than overmuch distortion of the labour market itself.

13 The Conduct of the Credit Base Condemned

Counter-Inflation Bill Second Reading; 5 March 1973

My Lords, the noble Lord, Lord Beswick, has announced that he will not ask his Party to divide against this Second Reading. If his decision had been otherwise, I confess that I should have gone into the Government Lobby. I should have gone into the Government Lobby, however, in a somewhat Laodicean frame of mind. I should go in not because I think in principle and in the long run statutory control of incomes is the best way of managing that sort of thing. On the contrary, I still hold the view that if aggregate national spending is held more or less commensurate with the increase in the value of the product then freely negotiated contracts are better.

Secondly, I should vote for the Government not because I am in favour of control of all prices. I am certainly in favour of control in the long period of some prices, prices which are, either necessarily or by way of conspiracy, monopolistically determined. But in general, trying to keep things in proper perspective, I am opposed to direct interference with the result of market forces. This is not because I think that the direct result of market forces is always a good thing, but because I think that, if it is not a good thing, it is far better to tackle the fundamental influences behind demand and supply, to tackle them by way of taxes or subsidies or even by physical controls, than to monkey about with prices, which, after all, are a result of these fundamental forces. I do not believe, therefore, that price control is a good thing in itself. I do believe that all historical experience since the time of Diocletian shows how likely it is to be ineffective and how likely it is to run into grave trouble.

The reason I support this Bill is otherwise. I support it because I believe it is the only hope of stopping the fundamental conditions of inflation without bringing about a major depression. And by 'a major depression' I do not mean the degree of depression that we have had lately, which has not been very much above the average which William Beveridge thought was the utmost achievable in his famous book on *Full Employment in a Free Society*. I mean rather old style, catastrophic unemployment, perhaps six, seven or even more per cent. I do not think we can get out of the truly terrible pickle in which we have got ourselves without such a disaster unless we are prepared to swallow a dose of the very disagreeable medicine which the Government at the moment are administering to us.

May I explain this attitude a little further. Inflation since the war is explained in many ways. It is sometimes explained in terms of demand, excessive spending on the part of someone or other; sometimes in terms of cost-push, successful monopolistic pressure for increased pay out of any relation to increased production. These explanations are very difficult to separate out. I have no doubt at all that in recent years there has been a considerable element of cost-push. I defy anyone to contend successfully that increases in earnings of 15 to 20 per cent bear any relation whatever to the movements of the gross national product in recent years. But at the same time I would point out that with a public spending deficit of the order of magnitude which threatens to emerge, cost-push is not the only influence. It is not the main influence, for instance, on the level of land prices, to which allusion has been made already.

Be this all as it may, it seems to me that the fundamental point to bear in mind is that these things, cost-push, or excess governmental spending, would not be likely to happen if the rate of increase in the credit base were no greater than the rate of increase in the value of production at constant prices. Of course it is possible to conceive that, for a time, this condition might be offset by some increase in the rate at which money is used— namely, by the creation of credit outside the main organised credit system or, as happens in times of severe crisis, by a rush to turn money into goods at any price. It seems to me that in the main the proposition is incontestable that if the rate of increase of spending power is not greater than the rate of increase of production, attempts to borrow in excess of the disposition to save will prove nugatory and attempts to push up incomes will simply leave more persons without work.

But what has actually happened? Since the end of June 1970, when the present Government came into office, M3—the most commonly accepted measure of the credit base—had increased to last September by something of the order of magnitude of 40 per cent. In the same period G.N.P. increased by—what shall we say?—5 per cent. I hope that noble Lords will notice that I am speaking in a loose way. I do not attach too much importance to precise figures here; I have handled too many of them myself. All sorts of things can go wrong in the best estimates; all kinds of incidental movements can be explained away by transitory circumstances. But surely the comparative orders of magnitude that I have cited are unmistakable. With that sort of disparity between the increase in the money stock and the increase of the national product, I would say that inflation of the kind that we have become accustomed to is inevitable.

It may be that some noble Lords on my left would regard it as unfair to take my figures from June 1970. Much the same sort of rate of increase in the money stock began in the last few months of the former Chancellor of the Exchequer, Mr Roy Jenkins. Having regard to the way in which his balance-of-payments troubles disappeared almost overnight when he had screwed himself up to reduce the rate of increase of aggregate spending, the change of policy has always been something quite astonishing to me. But June 1970, is a long time ago. The present Government have been in office more than two years, and one of their chief promises at the election was to arrest the rise of prices. Until recently, at any rate, with all respect, the rise of prices has not been arrested. I am an admirer of the present Chancellor of the Exchequer; I am a very great admirer of some of the financial reforms which he has instituted or, to take the case of negative income tax, which he has been the first Chancellor to contemplate; but I must say, in all humility, that looseness of his control of this very fundamental magnitude must be, in my opinion, a permanent blot on the record, and one for which the nation has had to pay very dearly. Look at what has happened to the balance of payments in recent months.

There are those who think that, given this sort of diagnosis, it follows that the problems could be solved quite simply by arresting the rate of increase of money supply until it had a more normal relationship to the increase of production. I wish that I could share that view, but I do not. Once inflation on the scale we have recently experienced is in full tide, a sudden check of the order of magnitude which would be necessary in increase of money stock would be likely to bring about a grave crisis. Once inflation is proceeding at that rate, all experience shows that business expectations and trade union expectations are keyed up to further increase. Wage claims are in the pipeline which take account of expectations of that sort. If the finance is not available and there occurs a sudden retardation of the rate of increase, then dismissals and bankruptcies are probable. Only if there is some artificial check on the increase of claims can we hope that production will continue at the present level, or perhaps even grow.

It is for this reason that I think that the general principle of that upper limit on pay increases for the time being is worth supporting. Not that I think that it will not involve injustices; most obviously it will. Not that I think that there will not be a good deal of evasion and that eventually it will crumble; I think that that will happen. But I think that it affords a breathing space, the only breathing space that I can conceive; a pause in which we can regain control of the increase of money stock without causing an industrial crisis, and an opportunity for the public to realise what many of them have long forgotten (as the noble Lord, Lord Byers, so vividly pointed out), that claims on G.N.P. which exceed its rate of increase by very much, such as those that we have recently witnessed, can only result in either inflation or unemployment.

As regards details, surely those are better discussed at the Committee stage. I have comparatively little to say about the pay provisions. I think that the attempt to bias negotiations in favour of the lower paid, put forward with the most excellent motives, may well prove self-defeating in that it will provide an obvious incentive to substitute skilled for unskilled labour. But the idea of a general upper limit beyond which increases are not an allowable cost—I am quoting from the explicit words of the White Paper rather than the Bill—seems to me to be sound. I confess to many more hesitations about price control. Here I find myself in considerable agreement with what was said by the noble Lord, Lord Byers. I think that we ought not to forget that where there is not strong monopolistic power, prices are results and not causes. As I said once before in your Lordships' House, the rise since 1930 in the value of my dwelling in the Hampstead Garden Suburb from about £3,000 to about £40,000 is a result, not a cause, of inflation. I am not a cause of inflation.

My Lords, I would urge that the adaptability of market prices to the underlying conditions of demand and supply is a valuable feature of any system, whether privately or publicly run. I think all experience shows that if prices are held at levels much below that which would clear the market, there tend to develop shortages, and distributions according to the time that people can afford to wait in queues rather than according to what they are prepared to pay. I must say that I think one can tremendously underestimate—I felt that the noble Earl, with whose general intentions I feel such tremendous sympathy, himself underestimated—the administrative difficulties which seem to me to leap to the eye from the most casual perusal of the Green Paper. No doubt in Committee we shall have more opportunity of alluding to these difficulties, but my imagination boggles when I think of the difficulties which will emerge in the definition of, for instance, what seems to be the simple concept of allowable cost. As I read the Bill and the Code, I must confess that I think there is real danger of upsetting the relative incentive to produce the things most in demand, and to contract those for which demand is less urgent.

As for the idea of controlling prices, including import prices, and leaving incomes to be determined in a free-for-all, hazy atmosphere of good will, I hope it is not necessary to point out that this is the road to further crisis, both national and private. The Government and nationalised industry would be committed to rising deficits and the private sector would be doomed to bankruptcy, unless indeed the influence of credit creation were to continue, and that could go on for only a limited time before a final crash. I say, in all earnestness, that those who suggest that the control of imported food prices is easy, should consider again the lessons of war experience. During the war, we succeeded in doing it by monkeying about with the index numbers and by putting all imports under State control, which I doubt whether many Members of your Lordships' House wish to do as a transitional measure. In fact, in point of pure logic—and I am not adhering to pure logic; I say that lest noble Lords on the Opposition side rise and charge me with being a cold-blooded economist, guided only by the geometry of his craft—if you are to have one kind of control rather than the other, it would be better to have pay control and let prices look after themselves.

Nevertheless I agree that government is the art of the possible, and since, I am sorry to say, at least 80 per cent of the population of this country, regardless of party, probably think that the levels of prices are determined not as they in fact are, in the main, by impersonal forces, but by the manipulations of profiteers and monopolists, I suppose we must stomach a certain amount of unnecessary price control to make the prevention of inflationary pay claims at all palatable. I would only predict that the price we pay for this palatability in its present form—I am not arguing that it is incapable of improvement—may be quite considerable. I am quite sure that if we succeed in getting the volume of aggregate demand into a more reasonable relation with aggregate production, it will be quite unnecessary to have control of prices over all that part of the field where any sort of competition prevails.

In all this, we must try to keep a sense of perspective. In a former debate, I remember that the noble Lord, Lord Platt, said that he wondered—I hope I did not mistake him—whether this is not a crisis of capitalism. I would rather say that it is a crisis of finance. It is not the existence of private enterprise which has got us into this muddle; on the contrary, the crisis, I am sorry to say, is most acute in nationalised industries, where the delusion prevails that the public purse is a sort of widow's cruise, and where, because of the pivotal nature of nationalised industries, most harm can be done to society when attempts are made to stop the process of excessive claims. But I do not want to end on a note of controversy. Rather I should hope that we would all agree that the essence of the trouble is an excess of aggregate demand over supply at stable prices, and that unless that excess is directly curbed no amount of restraint on pay and prices will prevent further trouble.

14 The Crisis in the Mines and Incomes Policy

Motion: Industrial and Economic Situation; 6 February 1974

My Lords, this afternoon we are debating a subject on which, as the very distinguished speeches which have already been made by representatives of the three parties demonstrate, there is considerable conflict of view. I am an humble cross-bencher and my thoughts on this subject do not run completely on the lines which have been adopted either by the distinguished speaker for the Government or the distinguished speaker for the Opposition. Perhaps I may be permitted in all candour to discuss the position as it presents itself to an isolated individual with no party affiliation, but one who has spent a considerable part of his life considering these questions of the overall equilibrium or disequilibrium of the economy.

First, let me make a few very banal remarks about inflation in general. In confronting this problem in general, and in drawing morals for what is to happen here and now in the crisis with which we are confronted, we have to bear in mind a fundamental proposition—an arithmetical banality, if you like—with regard to the relationship of spending and production. It is this: if the volume of spending on a national scale does not exceed the value of current domestic production for home consumption, plus the value of imports, then all will be well as regards the value of money and as regards the dangers of inflation. But, if the volume of expenditure exceeds that amount then, other things being equal, prices will rise and in all sorts of ways inflation will permeate the system.

One must always be cautious in using affectively toned words. I should not like to suggest to your Lordships that all inflation is intolerable. I think history shows that industrial countries can survive, although with a certain amount of friction, a rate of inflation of, let us say, $1\frac{1}{2}$ per cent per annum, 2 per cent per annum and, for short periods at any rate, a little more than that. But equally I think that rates of inflation such as have occurred in the last four years are not in the long run tolerable to societies such as ours. It may be that in Latin America, at the cost of a vast inroad into social relations and public morality, rates of inflation higher than the rates I have mentioned may be tolerated, year in, year out. But, frankly, I do not believe—and I imagine that this thought is shared by most of your

Lordships—that that sort of thing can go on year in, year out, without destroying this society.

If we are agreed on that, then there are two main ways of dealing with the problem. The first way, and the way which has been adopted in the last two or three years, is a control of prices and incomes. If under such a system the total of incomes is reduced to the value of domestic production plus imports, then sooner or later inflation stops. I do not say for a moment this can be done overnight, but certainly some progress could be made if the object of the policy were so to speak, a convergent series, the volume of income increasing more slowly and the volume of production eventually catching up with it.

My Lords, the second method of dealing with a situation of this sort is direct operation on the sources of expenditure, the imposition of taxes, the proceeds of which are not spent; or a more fundamental control of the basis of all expenditure, namely, the volume of money and credit, a diminution of the volume of borrowing, both public and private. If the money is not available, then in the end the excess demand for goods and services will cease. There one has, so to speak, the tedious arithmetic, the banalities of the subjects, and I apologise for reiterating them. Let me now come a little closer to reality.

My Lords, I personally doubt the long-term viability of statutory control of prices and incomes. I respect the views of those who think that it can succeed in the long run. That view has been argued adequately again and again in this House by noble Lords of more than one party, and I have made enough mistakes in my life to know that in differing from them I may be wrong. But my own belief is that while statutory control of prices and incomes may be effective for a time, in the end it puts strains on administration, on social relations and on the efficiency of industury, both private and public. Therefore, in the long run I believe that the solution to this problem is much more to be found in financial and monetary policy than in the adoption of these centralised and detailed controls of the hundreds of thousands of bargains made in regard to goods and services every month of the year. Nevertheless, as I have ventured to say to your Lordships' House on earlier occasions, I am certainly prepared to accept the statutory control of prices and incomes as a temporary measure.

The alternative which I prefer as a long-term policy, the control of the source of expenditure and borrowing money, may be a very harsh medicine if the inflation has already become very brisk, as it has here, and if expectations of business are already geared to a continuation of inflation. In such circumstances, the adoption of income control as a temporary measure seems to me to be not only admissible but wise. After all, past experience shows that prices and incomes controls do not break down immediately.

But there is one fundamental condition of success for policies of this sort, namely, that financial and monetary policy should be in harmony with such a policy. There should be no further feeding of excess expenditure from these sources. By this, I do not mean a sudden application of the fiscal and monetary brake which would clearly be folly; but I do mean a gradual reduction of deficit financing, a gradual reduction of the rate of increase of the money supply.

My Lords, this is not what has happened in the last few years. The cost inflation has been financed by the extension of the credit base. Let us face the fact that on the demand side there has been a policy, no doubt engendered by good will, of deficit financing which I think has no precedent in the financial history of this country, save in wartime. At the same time, the main indices of credit expansion have been expanding at a rate at which I defy anyone to believe that production can increase in this country or, indeed, in most other countries of the world. The result has been what would be expected, I would have said, on grounds of pure principle—a continuing inflation, not only as regards the cost of living but—and this is more irritating to a great many people—as regards property and so on.

What is more, and this has a two-edged moral it has meant an aggravation of our balance-of-payments difficulties. If the inflation had been less here, if there had been less pressure of demand on production resources to satisfy demand at home, then the troubles caused by the increase of prices abroad might have been met by more productive resources being turned by the ordinary pressures of the ordinary operation of the market to production for export, so diminishing our difficulties in that respect. Do not let us underestimate those difficulties. This Government inherited from their predecessors a balance-of-payments surplus of something of the order of £1,000 million. Before the oil trouble began, the deficit on current balance-of-payments account was approaching the order of £2,000 million, a switchover which surely is a matter of very great anxiety indeed.

What I have just been saying is pretty severe criticism of some, not all but some, of the policies which have been adopted by Her Majesty's Government. But what about attitudes elsewhere. I must confess I am in some doubt as regards the attitude of the Labour Opposition, and my perplexity is focused on the fact that I do not know whether they do or do not want a statutory incomes policy.

Certainly I have heard most eloquent pleas for such a policy from Labour benches in this House, and, as I say, I have treated them with respect. But I cannot refrain from noticing that the idea of a statutory prices and incomes policy, or incomes policy at least, is definitely repudiated by many of the leaders of the trade unions; if I am not mistaken it is repudiated by the Trades Union Congress itself. Those who make this repudiation seem to favour rather a free-for-all in the matters of the labour market.

Well, I can conceive of an argument being put up in favour of that point of view, even in regard to the present crisis, although this is not my view. But, I must ask, do those members of the Labour movement who repudiate a statutory incomes policy accept the corollary of a sufficient restriction of aggregate demand to prevent the free-for-all degenerating into an inflationary scramble? If they do accept it, then they must accept too, especially at the present time, a very considerable increase in taxation, not merely taxation of the very rich—that is not wholly, but very largely, a mirage; it means the taxation of most of us here; it means the taxation of people enjoying even smaller incomes, and it means, too, the most rigid control of the rate of increase of the credit base, which in the short run, at any rate, might lead to even higher rates of interest than prevail at present. If they do accept these things, I appeal to them to say so. If not, then do let us be clear that at the present time, in the present circumstances of this country, the free-for-all in the labour market means hyper-inflation—hyper-inflation on the Continental scale, and eventually—because these things all come to an end; the trees do not grow up to the sky forever—a new money to replace sterling. That is *not* a joke.

May I conclude (I have already spoken too long) by offering three reflections on the industrial dispute under consideration. The first point I want to make—and I hope it will not be thought I am a wicked man—is that in my judgment what has been revealed so far has meant an offer to the miners which is not by current standards ungenerous. I accept the view, which I think was implicit in what the noble Lord, Lord Beswick, said, and doubtless will be said by other noble Lords in the course of the debate, that you can argue until the cows come home about the exact percentage significance; but compared with settlements that have already been made under Stage 3, this is not an ungenerous offer. And, after all, Stage 3 is out of date; the oil producers have made it out of date. Stage 4, if it ever comes in, will have to be more rather than less severe. I ask the question, with all respect to those who ask us to extend understanding and compassion to the position of the miners: have they had a much better offer in the past, and how does the position compare with the position of those who have settled already under Stage 3?

[Baroness Gaitskell intervened to point out that the miners were bottom of the league in the European Economic Community with regard to wages.]

My Lords, I believe the noble Baroness, Lady Gaitskell is right, as she usually is. But I humbly submit that comparisons with other countries in Europe are irrelevant in this context because *in general* we are rather near the bottom of the European league. We are the poor members of the European Community. We have been overtaken by France, Germany and others. It is humiliating to read about our position in the table with regard to national income per head in relation to the position of other countries.

My second reflection is that this is a dispute in a nationalised industry. It is not a question of a dispute over the disposal of excess profits made by private enterprise. The employer in this case, in the last analysis, is the nation. In my salad days, I was a rather rabid young Socialist, and we used to say that if the means of production, distribution and exchange were nationalised the problem of industrial relations would evaporate. Well, we know better now. The last thing that I wish to do is to bring an indictment against the miners as a body, but unless the history of the negotiations revealed so far in the Press, through the media, and by the noble Lord, Lord Carrington, is utterly false, some of the leaders of the miners—I am not calling them 'Reds'; I am perfectly aware of the danger of exaggeration, particularly at this stage in this respect—have shown themselves absolutely unyielding. All expedients have been rejected.

My third reflection is that we would do well to remember the terrible troubles which are ahead if the strike goes on. The dislocation of industry which has followed the three-day week is absolutely nothing to what must be expected if the strike actually breaks out. There will be internal privations on a large scale, and external discredit. Great companies will go bankrupt or will have to be helped out by injections of bank credit, which will not make the control of inflation any easier. As I have said before, we shall be back in something like the position in which we found ourselves after the cancellation of Lend-Lease—more or less bankrupt without external assistance. But, alas! there is the additional complication that at the moment, with all the good will which is incipient in the atmosphere of this House, we are, let us face it, a divided nation. The temptation to settle, therefore, and to risk the consequences is very great.

That is all I have to say. I would only add that I agree with those who say that we must watch anxiously for any opportunity to break the hitherto unyielding attitude of those concerned. But—and this is the last thing I have to say—there are moments in the life of an individual, or in the life of nations, when we have to make fateful decisions. I think that I have made it clear that I do not completely admire the policy which has been pursued as regards public finance by the present Government in the last two years, and even more recently, but I am clear in this—the Queen's Government must be carried on.

15 The Significance of the So-called Social Contract Queried

Counter-Inflation (Abolition of Pay Board) Order 1974; 18 July 1974

My Lords, I am bound to confess that in the abstract the prospect of the operations of the Pay Board in the past have never filled me with great enthusiasm. I used to listen to a great many of my friends—and I have many of them in the Labour Movement—assuring me that the policy of full employment would not work if there were not some statutory control of prices and incomes. How often have I sat in this Chamber and heard the noble Lord, Lord Balogh, expatiating in terms to that effect. I myself have always been sceptical. I have looked at the verdict of history—and after all there is a good deal of history in the background of attempts of this sort in different countries, and so far as I can see they have always in the end broken down. Our own experience in that respect simply confirms that impression.

But I ask myself still: what purpose ought one to have in mind in considering the operations of this body; and if that purpose is not being fulfilled, what are the alternatives? So far as I can see, it would be perfectly futile to expect that an inflation of the order of magnitude that we are undergoing at the present time could possibly be cured by the operation of a prices and incomes policy—to use a slightly broader term—just like that. It is an extremely feeble instrument with which to cope with the powerful forces which are disrupting economic society here and in many other parts of the world at the present time.

However, I think that given good will and general acceptance, a pay policy at any rate might have the function of arresting the increase of unemployment. If a government are determined to tackle high inflation (if not hyper-inflation) by the only means by which it can be fundamentally eventually controlled—namely, by a tighter control on aggregate expenditure, either through the monetary or the fiscal weapon—then the existence of a pay policy, the existence of a policy which will prevent associations of producers putting up their demands at a time at which the rate of increase of aggregate expenditure is being reduced, would mean that there was less of a depression than otherwise would be the case.

For that reason when the last Government introduced their policies regarding pay, although I was always gloomily sceptical I was prepared to pay lip service to the desirability of making the attempt. I do not know of any case in history where an inflation of the order of magnitude that we are suffering at the moment has been eventually arrested without causing a certain amount of depression. It seems to me that if the brakes were put on, as it was desirable that they should be put on, then the existence of such a policy might mitigate the difficulties.

The last Government certainly did not do that. The last Government pursued utterly contradictory policies. They attempted to control prices and incomes directly, but at the same time they let the volume of aggregate expenditure go rip. While it was ridiculous to hope that the gross national product should increase by more than 6 per cent, let us say, in the last twelve months of the Conservative Government, the credit base, the famous 'M3', was increasing by something of the order of magnitude of 25 per cent. No prices and incomes policy in the world will arrest disaster if the volume of purchasing power released by such an increase in the credit base meets a diminutive increase in the value of production of that order of magnitude. So we got, and are getting and will get for the next few months at any rate, a continuation of a most disturbing rate of inflation.

I have no particular love for the policies pursued by the present Chancellor of the Exchequer but, credit where credit is due, either the Chancellor of the Exchequer or the Bank of England have succeeded in reducing the rate of increase of the credit base. Whereas under the last Government the credit base was increasing by a rate of something like 25 per cent per annum, it has now been reduced to something more like 16 per cent per annum. A very sharp reduction, a very sharp application of the brakes, if I may say so; an application which I should expect to find in the months to come if he persists in it (which I suspect he will not) accompanied by some diminution of economic activity and eventually perhaps by some diminution of the increase in prices.

My Lords, what is going to happen in the future? This is the important point, and the point which, after all, is raised acutely in the statement by the noble Lord, Lord Shepherd. The rate of increase of aggregate expenditure has been substantially reduced. Now, supposing that this gives rise, as it certainly will give rise, to some diminution of industrial activity, to the emergence of some unemployment; and supposing at the same time, the Pay Board having been dissolved, there are claims here and there for rates of increase incompatible with the norm laid down by the noble Lord, Lord Shepherd. In that case, I submit that if the present policy of monetary and fiscal restraint is adhered to, there will be more unemployment than there would have been otherwise.

What are our defences against that? Noble Lords on all sides have talked about a social contract, or a social compact. As I sat here, I must say I was mystified. I have been away in different parts of the world from time to time during this session, and I wondered whether I had missed the issue of some important White Paper. Then I recalled an article which I read in *Private Eye* the other day, about the discovery of the Social Contract in a bookshop in Reading by an old lady turning over a parcel of secondhand books. I wondered whether there does in fact exist a contract in any intelligible sense of the world, if it is used in a constitutional or other stricter meaning. So far as I can see, 'social compact' is simply a pious hope that everyone will behave nicely, and that somehow or other a more decent form of society will be evolved. This is a hope which I share.

Meanwhile what are you going to do if the austerity in aggregate expenditure continues and there is a slackening in the volume of employment? What are you going to do if at the same time some trade unions infringe the norm which has been laid down by the noble Lord, Lord Shepherd? Are you going to see more unemployment, or are you going to reverse the fiscal engines again, and land us still further in the international mess which overhangs the Western world at the present time to a degree few of us in this Chamber, I fear, fully realise?

16 Advocacy of Reflation Absurd with Prices Rising at 20 per cent per annum

Financial Bill Second Reading; 30 July 1974

My Lords, the Motion of the noble Lord, Lord Carrington, raises essentially controversial issues. It is a matter of congratulation for your Lordships' House that these controversial issues have so far been dealt with in the spirit of mutual toleration and sweet reasonableness which characterises our debates and which in my opinion is a clinching argument for this House's perpetuation. I think it true to say that all those who have spoken so far have in greater or less degree agreed upon one point—that the situation with which we are confronted is grave. Perhaps the term 'grave' is strong for one or two of the speeches to which we have listened, but I imagine in the hearts of most of us at this moment there is a degree of anxiety concerning the future of this country, at any rate in the next two or three years, probably greater than has existed at any time since the war. Reference has been made in the course of observations to the various crises which have occupied our attention from time to time in the last 25 years. Those crises were 'chicken-feed' compared to the problems which confront us at the present day.

Consider for a moment the quantitative aspect of the situation. We are informed by that sedate and sober body OECD that prices are likely to rise at the rate of 20 per cent per annum in this country. There is a prospect—I will not say more—that costs may rise even more. Our balance of payments, if we include the oil payments (and there is no reason for excluding them), is running at a truly alarming rate. Even the betterment to which the noble Lord, Lord Beswick, referred indicates a state of affairs which cannot go on for ever and which cannot for ever be sustained by borrowing from the Shah or from more anonymous lenders who have shown themselves willing to support sterling up to date. At the same time—and in some respects this is the new and puzzling feature of the situation—the inflation is already beginning to show its evil effects. The cash flow of companies, their resources of liquidity, have been eroded.

Rates of interest are abnormally high because you can fool some of the lenders some of the time but you cannot fool all of them all of the time, and once they have 'twigged' that inflation is going on at anything like the rate at which it has been proceeding in the last few years, interest rates are bound to rise if only to compensate. That in turn produces its effect on the Stock Exchange, on investment, and so on.

How has all this come about? Why is it that this community, so abounding in good will and decency and improvement on all sides compared to what it was in my young days or even 25 years ago, has got itself into this pickle? I often think as I read speeches by prominent personalities—I will not specify of what political affiliation—that the impression is widely diffused that this is some spontaneous evil, something which has come about as, for instance, the emergence of a new influenza virus might afflict us, a new virus for which for the time being no immunisation had been discovered. But, my Lords, this is not so. Generalisations about mysterious forces which affect the ups and downs of society from time to time may have something in them, but so far as I know they have never been demonstrated. The mysterious, impersonal forces may exist, but we do not know much about them and in my judgment it is not necessary to invoke their existence to explain where we are at the present time.

> The fault, dear Brutus, is not in our stars,
> But in ourselves, that we are underlings.

We all know that inflation is going on in different parts of the world—this of course is the pretext for the exponents of the theory of what I call the collective virus. But inflation is going on in different parts of the world at different paces. Further, while external inflation is clearly an embarrass-ment for countries which try to exclude themselves from it, some degree of exclusion is not at all out of the question. Why is it, my Lords, that the Federal Republic of Germany, drastically defeated in the Second World War, is now the strongest economy in Europe? Why is it that the decline in the value of the mark since the new mark was introduced after a disastrous hyperinflation, has been much less than has been the decline here. Certainly they did not start with any advantage. Nobody who is acquainted with the circumstances of Germany before the currency reform can possibly believe that they had a flying start for the economic miracle.

My Lords, I think that it is worth dwelling a moment longer upon this question of varying rates of inflation. What should a country do which finds itself surrounded by inflation or rising prices due to real causes in other parts of the world? What should a country do if the terms of trade turn drastically against it, as they have done in our case? With a drastic turn in the terms of trade against a country, there is clearly a situation of considerable embarrassment. In real terms it means that for the time being the amount that one can take out of the world dividend is less than otherwise it would have been.

Now what should be the remedy for a country which finds itself in that position? I do *not* say that it should drastically deflate, but it should, at any rate, moderate the existing rate of growth of general spending; and, of course, in present circumstances, if the internal aggregate expenditure is kept advancing but slowly or is stable then, with a floating rate, that can eventually put right the imbalance in the balance of payments. However, we have done just the opposite to that. In these circumstances, in the last few years we have inflated rather more than other people. Therefore, it is not at all surprising that we have landed ourselves in ever-increasing difficulties.

My Lords, I am prompted to leave the tenor of the remarks which I had planned by an observation by my great friend the noble Lord, Lord Boyle, who, by implication, if I may say so, slightly misrepresented the attitude which I adopt in addressing your Lordships' House. May I assure the noble Lord, Lord Boyle, that I am not a Friedmanite monetarist. I do not believe in tying one arm behind my back when coping either with inflation or with deflation.

While I should be sorry to be thought to be saying that there was not an element of demand inflation in what has happened in this country during the last two or three years, of course I freely admit that some of it has been due to cost inflation. On that point—and I submit that it is not an academic or subtle point—it is one thing to say that one cannot fight cost inflation and reduce cost inflation by active monetary measures (which I should not necessarily say) and another thing to say that cost inflation is much less likely to take place if the supply of money is not over-elastic. On that latter position, certainly I take my stand, in part, at any rate, as an explanation of the events of the last few years. But certainly I do not take the view of Mr Enoch Powell who says that the demands of various associations of producers have got absolutely nothing to do with what has happened and that it is solely the Government's business to maintain the integrity of money. Life is more complex than that, and it is quite easy to understand how Governments, faced with the unemployment which might result from containing the money supply in the face of cost inflation, have been willing to give way (in my judgment, too much) to what has been happening.

Addressing myself now to the question of practical policy in this respect, May I say in all candour that I think that the policy which was pursued by the late Government up to the cuts of just before Christmas 1973 was a policy which contained fundamental inconsistencies. I myself think that while incomes policies usually break down in the long run and are attended by the greatest complications, yet it was certainly worth while trying an incomes policy; and certainly it can be defended on the ground that if an incomes policy is successful it tends to reduce unemployment. My apology for the adoption of an incomes policy in such a situation as one had, say, at the beginning of 1973, would be much more that if one were trying to contain inflation by fiscal and monetary measures, if an incomes policy were in operation there would be less unemployment than otherwise would be the case. However, as we all know, the late Government—actuated, I am sure, by courage and public spirit—at once imposed an incomes policy and proceeded to indulge in deficit financing on a scale not known before in peacetime; and the result, I am sure, was predictable. It has, indeed, been predicted in this House by various individuals.

My Lords, that Government has passed now, and one has to ask oneself what is one to expect of the policy of the present Government. I am not at all in love in all sorts of ways with the general policies of the present Chancellor of the Exchequer. Some of these have been mentioned, and others have not been mentioned. However, I think that credit should be given to the Government and to the Bank of England for containing the rate of increase of money supply—indeed, for bring it down at a speed which some monetarists would argue is likely to bring about effects which otherwise might have been avoided later on. These things act with time-lags, and a frequent time-lag is anything up to eighteen months. While I do not believe in the quantification of these things—too much quantification is bogus—the existence of time-lags is something which we all ignore at our peril. So far, so good; but in the meantime we have abolished the Pay Board. We abolished it last week. Although, as the noble Lord, Lord Beswick, reminded us, there will be coming into being an apparatus for arbitration and conciliation, it is no exaggeration to say that at present the prospect is one of a more or less 'free-for-all' in the market services. If that free-for-all explodes, then either the financial policy of the Government, of containing the credit base and the rate of increase of expenditure is undermined, or there is real unemployment and a substantial depression.

While wishing with all your Lordships to see a ray of hope on the horizon, I must confess that I share the private gloom which was expressed in the columns of the *Sunday Telegraph* last Sunday by my friend and colleague, the noble Lord, Lord Kahn. I feel gloomy about what is going to happen on the wages front in the next 12 months. I come from considering this morning a demand from an extremely nice and respectable body of people for an increase of 27 per cent, which is certainly an increase far transcending the norm laid down by the Trades Union Congress or that announced from the Government front bench last week by the noble Lord, Lord Shepherd, when he explained to us that it is the wish of the Government that increases in wages in the coming year should not be more than will maintain constant the existing standards of living.

What is the climate of opinion at the present time regarding this rather grave situation? I fancy that if there were some intelligent visitor from another planet, or even if we were visited by one of the gnomes of Zurich—one of the intelligent gnomes—he would be quite astonished at finding the columns of the newspapers, and a good deal of private discussion, preoccupied with the question of whether we should reflate on a massive scale with prices predicted by the OECD to rise at the rate of 20 per cent per annum. I have no doubt at all that the curtailment of the rate of increase of the credit base and the reduction of the extravagant borrowing will bring depression—it always does—and, certainly, it is the ideal objective of an incomes policy to reduce that depression to a minimum. But in the present state of affairs I am bound to say that the absence of control—although perhaps control was bound to break down—is likely to make matters worse.

Yet it seems to me that to go very far in the direction of reflation at this moment would certainly, ultimately, run the danger of there occurring something even worse than that. It would be bad enough to start reflating on any large scale if we were a closed economy. It might be mitigated by more index number devices, and so on, but it would be bad enough. But in our position we must remember that we are internationally vulnerable. Even if you leave aside the payments which have to be made for oil and focus attention on the rest, the adverse balance of payments is formidable and will certainly take some time to work off, even with the most austere policy.

In this connection, I might say that the existence of a floating rate is really no ultimate safeguard against the troubles which might be caused if the internal policy were to bring it about that trust in sterling was undermined. If sterling were to float downwards now in a burst of no confidence—and that is always possible even although we have in the kitty all sorts of promises of support and loans, and so on—it would not reassure people for long if they thought we were simply frittering it away on a reflationary policy. But a downward movement of sterling on any large scale at the moment would certainly affect us disadvantageously in more than one way. It would first increase the cost of imports and would therefore have a tendency, at any rate, to ginger up the wages spiral; and, secondly, as it proceeded, even despite the foreign backing, it would tend to increase the danger of a real run on sterling just at the time when we most needed to sustain confidence.

I will not say that in a year or two's time we may not need to take more risks; we may not need some reflation. The extent will depend, to some extent, on the degree of unemployment which has been caused by excessive income settlements in the meantime. But that date is still distant. The only plausible case for acting before then would be if one could assume that a more or less total incomes freeze imposed from now on, behind which there could perhaps be manipulations of a degree much greater than those dared by the present Chancellor of the Exchequer to revive the failing confidence in industry and to give a stimulus to invention. But does anyone in his senses believe that such a policy is immediately practicable, whatever the vicissitudes of fortune may cause us to do later on? For the time being, for months, and I suspect a year or two ahead, we must endure some degree of recession caused by the errors of the past if something worse is not to happen. The question is, have we the will? In the last resort, there is a moral side to the confusion which affects public affairs at the present time. It is a test of the system of self-government, of which we are so proud. People have not been told, with the degree of candour that they deserve, the degree of danger in which they stand.

My Lords, at present my pessimistic verdict is that if the people were told they had a choice between some degree of recession or a perpetuation of inflation, many of them would say: 'Get on with the inflation'. But that cannot persist. At its present rate of depreciation, the value of sterling will be halved in less than five years. While the Latin American countries may stand that sort of disturbance, I am quite sure that our more complex and delicately poised society cannot. Sooner or later, the conception of trade-off will change and people will say: 'For heaven's sake, stop the inflation no matter what the disagreeable side-effect!' I hope it will be sooner rather than later. If not, I tremble to think of the convulsions this splendid society of ours, with its glorious past, may have to undergo.

17 Pay Restraint and 'Monetarism'

Motion: The Attack on Inflation; 30 July 1975

My Lords, since we last debated the economic situation we have had a glimpse into the abyss. There was a Monday a few weeks ago when the official slogan still was 'no panic'. A day or two after that, a statement was issued showing the utmost apprehension. Now we have this document which is the subject of discussion today and of a Bill which we shall be discussing tomorrow. I accept the exortation of the noble Lord, Lord Feather, in that I would wish to avoid cynicism in this respect. I would concede that what we have to discuss at least shows an awareness of danger and some willingness to cope with it. Moreover, it cannot be said too frequently that the period of intense danger has ceased, but if anything goes seriously wrong with the present policy, the alarm which gave rise to the statement and what has succeeded it might easily be reawakened. Therefore, even if one has very considerable reservations about this policy and its future—as, indeed, I have—it is desirable this evening to choose one's words very carefully and to say nothing to make things more difficult for the fine men at the Bank of England who are fighting against possible catastrophe for us and our children. Also, I would urge that nothing should be said to impair any possible solidarity among men of good will in grappling with the problems of the future, and discussing them with candour and some detachment.

My Lords, the chief feature of the White Paper is quite clearly the restraints on incomes. Whether you think this is a voluntary or statutory incomes or pay policy is a matter for argument, and so too, let us admit, are some of the proposed instruments for bringing about this policy. But beyond that the general principle involved has provoked some general discussion, alluded to in the distinguished speech of the noble Lord, Lord Boyle of Handsworth. I submit that that degree of generality deserves some attention. I will confess to your Lordships that I do not share the belief expressed in many speeches this evening from both sides of the House that a permanent statutory control of incomes and policy over the wide field of the economy has necessarily come to stay. Statutory control of incomes and prices in peacetime has never so far lasted for very long, and has seldom been successful; it is apt to breed a sense of injustice and resentment. This

84

process, at any rate in the past, has tended to be cumulative, and eventually there has come some sort of breakdown. Whether or not Mr Jones's £6 maximum per week is enough, whether it is going to succeed or not, we can be quite sure that before the year is out it will have bred a whole crop of problems, and that the policy of re-entry, as the noble Lord who introduced the debate described it, will not be unattended by trouble. Thus, in general, I differ from my friends who argue that a permanent overall pay and prices policy is desirable. I would certainly urge—and here I hope I should gain support from some who disagree with what I have just said—that if a prices and incomes policy is used as an excuse for refraining from other measures it will simply be an *ignis fatuus*.

Having said that, I would urge that there are circumstances in which an overall incomes policy or pay policy is of use. If you are in a situation when attempts are in some way or other being made to curb inflation by reducing excess expenditure, and if at that moment there arise demands for increases of pay which are not justified by increased productivity, then the result certainly will be business failure, redundancies and unemployment. But if at such a time there is, for the time being at any rate, a measure of restraint in the increase of incomes, the resulting unemployment will not be so great. More people will be employed at the same level of expenditure. In my submission, this is just our position at the present day.

We are undergoing a process of inflation unprecedented in our peace-time history, and if it goes on at the present rate undoubtedly it will eventually tear our society apart. And what is a much more immediate danger, it will destroy our international position and all that depends on that in the next five years or so. According to the Chancellor of the Exchequer, who, I confess, is not my favourite statistician, 5 per cent of the national income is sustained by foreign creditors. So we really must do something about the inflation. We cannot allow it to continue on the present scale. We must curb the rate of increase of expenditure.

My Lords, let us face it, it is highly improbable that this can be done without some increase of unemployment. I do not believe that an inflation of this order of magnitude has ever been curbed in history without a considerable increase of unemployment. Unemployment is already a matter of concern. It is not yet 5 per cent, but 5 per cent is a matter of concern. If at such a time there are demands for more pay of the order of magnitude of the demands we have seen granted during recent history, I see no escape whatever from a further increase in unemployment of formidable proportions. In some way or other, therefore, I conclude that restraint of pay claims is the only way of mitigating this very grave social evil. I do not see any avoiding this conclusion.

Those whose preoccupation is with the volume of unemployment rather than with the rate of inflation, which is perhaps a legitimate occupation although not one that I share, may say that we should not curb the rate of expenditure, we should spend more in order to mop up the unemployment that already exists. But if we spend more in the aggregate, if at this moment we reflate—the fashionable word—then the inflation will go on, and, apart from the deplorable internal consequences, we cannot prevent some withdrawal of foreign funds, we cannot prevent the cessation of the foreign lending on which a comparatively easy passage through our present difficulties depends. So I would say that the broad justification of the present policy of pay restraint is just this, that it prevents the rise in unemployment being as great as it otherwise would be, if adequate steps are taken to arrest inflation.

What steps are adequate? Here we enter a field where I think sensible discussion has been much befogged by quite unnecessary intrusion of technicality, and some blame, no doubt, attaches to academics for the diffusion of these misunderstandings. The noble Lord, Lord Boyle, delivered a forceful and interesting criticism of the ambiguous attitude which he described as 'monetarism'. I will come to his remarks on that matter in a moment. But to start with, let me state what surely will be agreed to be an unimpeachable platitude; namely, that inflation takes place when the volume of spending exceeds the volume of goods available or potentially available at constant prices. That is so simple there could be no dispute about it.

But I think it is equally true, although doubtless this is a controversial subject, that the excess of aggregate expenditure cannot long continue if the ultimate supply of purchasing power—notes and bank credit and so on—does not increase, or does not increase much, beyond the rate at which the volume of goods and services available at constant prices is increasing. All historical experience sustains that simple view. You can have periods, shortish periods, in which people will not spend at the usual rate, when they think that prices are going to fall. You can have periods when they spend at more than the usual rate because they think inflation is going to go on. But if the money supply does not increase more than commensurately with the volume of goods and services available at constant prices you will not get continuing inflation.

I think the confusion to which the noble Lord, Lord Boyle, was alluding has been aggravated by the discussion of causes and culprits. Some people have said that demands for extra pay cannot cause inflation if the money supply is looked after in a proper way. That is certainly said during the debates in the other place. And perhaps in a sense that is true. But in a world in which governments have an eye on the volume of employment as well as on the price level, it is very easy indeed to see that if there are calls for excessive pay increases in some parts of the system then there will be a temptation to a compensatory increase in money supply to prevent the causation of unemployment.

I therefore think that it is highly paradoxical for my friend Milton Friedman to say that all inflation is caused by monetary influences, just like that. If that is what is meant by a repudiation of monetarism, I certainly would not call myself a monetarist, and certainly would repudiate supplementing monetary policy with fiscal policy, or even—what would be much less popular in certain quarters—anti-monopoly policy. But if monetarism means simply that inflation, however initiated, whoever the culprit, cannot go on if the rate of increase of money supply is held properly in check, then certainly I modestly admit to that degree of monetarism.

Descending from these abstract considerations, which I apologise for inflicting on your Lordships' House, to our present situation, it is true that the rate of increase of money, either M1 or M3, has been considerably reduced during the lifetime of the present Government compared with the excesses of an earlier period. But since this sort of thing operates only with a pretty long time lag, and the change in the rate of increase itself takes time to seep through, I opine that there is still a considerable amount of incipient inflation in the system. This is a case where the evil that men do lives after them. Whether or not it is possible to bring the rate down to 10 per cent by this time next year is, to me, an open question. I do not believe that economic science provides any sure ground for confident prediction either way.

Let me ventilate a further apprehension. One of the influences on the rate of increase of money supply—because we are not talking about diminution; no one in his senses has talked about diminution in the absolute money stock; it is the second differential that one is talking about all the time—may be the borrowing requirement of government. Government borrowing need not lead to inflation if the disposition to save is sufficiently strong. But frequently it is not strong enough, and the borrowing which is thought to be necessary is financed by the creation of money, and that creation is necessarily inflationary—at any rate, in circumstances like the present.

At the present time, our borrowing requirement, partly because of the effects of inflation itself, has increased out of all knowledge. Figures given by the Chancellor of the Exchequer in his Budget Statement were such as to make one's hair stand on end, and since that event I should guess that the borrowing requirement has risen even further. Therefore, the fear must arise in the minds of all reasonable people that unless we continue to get considerable help from abroad borrowing requirements of the present orders of magnitude must lead to the new creation of money, must lead to a renewal of the inflationary influences on that side. It is here that the White Paper, by itself, gives less reassurance than might have been hoped for. We are not told the targets as regards the rate of increase of M1 or M3. We are not told in the White Paper what the borrowing programme is likely to be. It is just here that those on whose good will we depend in the next few months, or even years, will be paying the most attention to the details of policy.

18 Persistence of Apprehensions and Deficit Financing

Debate on Address (Second Day); 20 November 1975

My Lords, may I address my limited remarks to the speech made from the Government benches, by the noble Lord the Lord Privy Seal. As may be expected, this was a forceful, lucid and candid speech, and it contained many utterances, some as asides, with which one could feel in complete agreement. I doubt whether many of us in this House would disagree with his emphasis that inflation was the main problem. I suspect, however, that he worked the overseas misfortunes rather too hard. There is no doubt the world is undergoing a recession more severe than we have experienced since the War. But the rest of the world has a fairly good prospect of recovery, and our prospects are not all that robust as things go at the moment. What must never be forgotten—and I hope is never forgotten by ministers responsible for policy—is that our position fundamentally is far worse than the position of the other industrial powers of the Free World. Inflation here has been four times as great as that in Germany and, at the present time, is very substantially greater than in the United States of America.

I also thought that the noble Lord the Lord Privy Seal was much too sanguine in the note on which he ended: that we were now on the right track and that if only the policies enumerated in the gracious Speech were followed we could look back on the past with horror, and with some anticipation and relief in the future. I doubt whether things are as simple as that. But, first, let me recognise the extent to which things have changed just a little for the better since we looked over the precipice in the summer.

I am sure that no one in this House would wish to underestimate the degree to which most of the leaders of the great trade unions have moved towards some degree of realistic appreciation of the pickle in which we find ourselves. I echo the praise which has been given to the initiative of Mr Jack Jones, although I must confess that I think the simple solution which he suggested has laid up a rod in pickle for those who try to negotiate the next settlement as regards wage policy. Secondly—here I may appear to some Members of your Lordships' House to be somewhat perverse—I

would not take too gloomy a view of the fact that we have now had recourse
to a loan from the International Monetary Fund. It may well be that that is
a sign that enthusiasm for lending on the part of other possible sources of
borrowing has waned, and it would be interesting to hear some indication
of how long this loan is likely to last.

I am quite sure that the present Chancellor of the Exchequer—that
great authority on statistics—must keep on his desk some indication of
future cash-flow. Although doubtless it would be too much to ask him to
put a date on the exhaustion of this charge, if it is anticipated that it may be
exhausted, it would be interesting to know whether it will last a month,
three months, a year, and so on. But I share a certain restricted satisfaction
over the fact that we are likely to get from the officials of the I.M.F.—
even at the present time when the conditions attached to this loan are not
particularly onerous—advice on how to deal with inflation which, having
regard to the mistakes made by both parties in the past, may be perhaps
beneficial.

So up to that point I can see just a ray of hope here and there, but I
confess I do not understand the suggestion which I think was implicit in the
speech of the noble Lord the Lord Privy Seal; that is, that there is any
strong light at the end of the tunnel, the way we are going now. The present
situation, certainly, is not one which gives rise to any satisfaction. Inflation
has been running for the last 12 months at about 25 per cent. The balance
of payments is still alarmingly adverse, whatever the causes of that
adversity may be, and, after all, there is a great deal of money in London,
which has been kept here in one way or another by the blandishments of
the extremely able men who manage our finances there, which might take
wing in a crisis. And although I have no doubt at all that in recent weeks
and months the rate of exchange has been to some extent sustained by
expenditure by the Bank of England, we must realise that it is now only just
over 2 dollars to the pound, which is not anything to be particularly proud
of when one compares it with earlier days.

Of course, the inference to be drawn from the speech of the noble Lord
the Lord Privy Seal was that a good deal of that is, so to speak in the past
and that perhaps the main problem is to see that unemployment does not
rise excessively. Apart from that, the rate of inflation is diminishing, the
rate of price increases is slowing down and the Chancellor of the Exchequer
has promised that the rate of inflation will be down to 10 per cent by the
autumn of next year.

My Lords, for a moment, let us suppose that that is true. Intrinsically I
do not think it conveys ultimate comfort to us, either in our capacity as
citizens or in our capacity as competitors in world markets. Should the rate
of inflation come down to 10 per cent, it will still mean that all those—and
there may be some in your Lordships' House—who depend on fixed
incomes will be losing, in addition to what they have already lost, 10 per
cent of the value of their money. Moreover, in that wished-for position next

autumn, in all probability, our costs will still be ahead of those of our competitors. We must always remember that the increase of £6 per head per week often, at least in many branches of activity, represents more than a 10 per cent increase in costs. With the best will in the world, and conscious of my position on the cross-benches here, I must confess that it does not seem to me that most of the legislation which has been occupying the attention of your Lordships' House in the last session suggests to the, mind progress towards great industrial efficiency, greater mobility of labour, fewer restrictive practices and fewer other evils which, in addition to inflation, have contributed to the troubles of recent years.

Equally with other speakers, I must confess to a sense of profound disappointment at the tone of and the suggestions in parts of the gracious Speech. It is all very well to talk about the splendid achievements at Chequers, the nature of which, apart from certain abstract sentences, is still concealed from us. The fact is—and I feel confident that this is right—that in this respect the gracious Speech will cause great despondency and create doubt among just those sections of the business community, and particularly the younger end of the community, which we should most wish to enlist in an industrial revival.

This is really not a matter which should be blinked at by the Government—that of your managers, not all of whom are superbly efficient but some of whom do an honest day's work, some 50 per cent, I would dare to say, are doubtful and apprehensive of the future, and of the future as regards Government policy. Speaking as one who spends a good deal of his life among younger people, I would say that many people would be surprised at the number of the really clever ones—the ones who really have an aptitude for business management and so on—who are quietly thinking of going away. This may be wrong, but if one of these young people were to come to me, while I should represent all sorts of reasons which make this country rather a nice place to live in, I should feel myself fraudulent if I were to give him an assurance that we were going to get out of our present troubles.

Doubtless there will be some relief of our position as the rest of the world revives; and I am fairly confident that, barring political accidents, which are always possible, it is likely to revive next year. But never let us forget that we have a long way to catch up. I have in my notes: 'How does productivity per million of investment here compare with elsewhere?' I need not emphasise that question. The answer was in fact furnished by the noble Lord, Lord Shepherd, himself. It compares very badly. That is a long period problem, but the problems of the short period are still with us.

To me, the most alarming feature of the short period is the magnitude of our deficit financing. It may be that the lessons which can be derived from contemplation of an uncontrolled money supply, such as occurred at certain phases in the history of the Conservative Government, have been learnt. I am not here urging the pure milk of monetarists' work or anything of that kind; I am simply alluding to the simple proposition that if there is not some upper limit on the rate of increase of the money supply, inflation is bound to follow. It may be that we have learnt that. Certainly the rate of increase of money supply has been diminished. But the deficit financing goes from bad to worse. I wonder by how many billions the deficit this financial year is going to exceed the estimate of the deficit given by the Chancellor of the Exchequer when he introduced his Budget in another place? This itself is a grave burden for the future, particularly at present rates of interest. But surely it is more alarming for the success of the anti-inflation policy.

I know that there is a very short-period answer to that question. It may be said, perhaps with justice, that at present the deficit financing is no threat to the anti-inflation policy. It may be said that people do not know what to do with their money; they are fed up and dispirited and leaving their money liquid simply becuase they do not know what to do with it. In such circumstances it may be argued, and argued with a certain cogency, that it should be possible to raise the money to finance the deficit without undue enlargement of the credit base, however it is measured. But what if a little recovery comes? The position will not be so sanguine then. We are told that industry is in so much need of extra investment. Is industry to be starved of investment because economic activity is greater? Is there not a real danger, while deficit financing continues at its present level, of further recourse, some months ahead perhaps, to an increase in the rate of inflation, particularly from a practical point of view if the persistent unemployment at its present level—and I think it is bound to rise—creates rising pressure for so-called reflation, which I am sure we here all agree would be premature?

So I confess that, despite recognition of some more favourable, or less unfavourable, elements in the situation, when I look round I see little but a series of unsolved problems. I therefore return to the central problem of all which is still, as the Lord Privy Seal said, that of containing inflation, and of inflation continuing at a greater rate than elsewhere. I ask: Do ministers seriously believe that with measures no sterner than those which are being applied at present our rate of inflation after the autumn of 1976 will be no greater than that of the United States or Germany?

In conclusion, my Lords, I ask myself what can be said in a constructive way apart from the standard exhortations to prune expenditure, abstain from measures which militate against general inflation and so on and so forth, of which we have heard a great deal this evening. May I preface my concluding remarks and recommendation by taking your Lordships for the moment into the stratosphere of high fantasy. There is a group of extremely reputable European economists, one from each of the nine countries, including a very clever professor of economics from the University of Manchester, who have in recent weeks published a manifesto in which they recommend that the authorities of the Nine should issue a new currency, the Europa, and—this is the catch—that we should all be allowed to use it as an alternative.

I have no doubt at all that if this were done, and if the Europa were being managed so as to hold promise of a constant purchasing power, there would be a real safeguard against inflation for individuals just as there would be, let me say in passing, if we were all allowed now to make our payments or contracts in Swiss francs; it is only because of rigid exchange control that the present unequal rates of inflation which prevail in the world can be contained. I have no doubt at all that if there were that degree of freedom, or if there were this issue of Europas under this condition, governments would be compelled to undertake a greater degree of financial prudence on pain of seeing their own currencies disappear from use altogether.

As I said, that is an excursion into the realm of high fantasy. Governments would be against such a limitation of their freedom of action to inflate and it may very well be that central banks might enter some caveat. But I seriously think—and this is my one positive suggestion for dealing with the problem caused by the abnormal deficits—that we should do well to look at some extension of the device of indexed government bonds.

This is not—I repeat 'not'—an endorsement of indexation in general which I have come to believe carries with it, if generalised, certain dangers which have not been recognised in recent discussion, particularly for a country in a position such as ours where the terms of trade are apt to turn against us and where, therefore, indexation would be a positively inflationary influence. But indexation of government borrowing is not in the same category as general indexation; it is simply an undertaking by governments to maintain intact the real value of what they borrow. I have no doubt that if it could be introduced the relief to savers would be extraordinary and the easement of non-inflationary borrowing considerable. I will conclude by saying that if it were introduced it would put an end to the monstrous fraud of asking uninformed people to lend at negative rates of interest, which is what still happens today.

My Lords, do the trees in this country grow up to the sky? All one's instincts, all one's affiliations, press one to say, No. Yet I cannot help thinking that the prospect would be more hopeful if there were more of us who would be prepared to admit that it might happen.

19 A Lack of Foreign Confidence

Motion: The Economic Situation; 9 June 1976

My Lords, today, the subject is the current crisis and, on that, although I recognise that many of the splendid speeches which have been delivered in your Lordships' House this afternoon have covered the main points, it may perhaps be worthwhile picking out one or two salient features of the immediate past and looking forward just a little to the future. A no less serious-minded and experienced person than the Prime Minister himself has argued that what happened before the splendid rescue operation was, so to speak, a manifestation of merely perverse influences. The pound was undervalued, said the Prime Minister, and, on the basis of that assertion, he seemed to convey the impression that anything which had happened to it in the past few weeks was necessarily completely irrational.

Undervaluation is a technical term. It arises from the comparison of what the noble Lord, Lord Cobbold, described as purchasing power parities—comparisons between prices and costs at home and abroad. I have no doubt at all that, as a matter of arithmetic, the Prime Minister was correct about the position which existed a few weeks ago and which exists at the present time, *pro tem*, but unless other things are all completely equal, purchasing power parities have comparatively little relation to demand and supply in the exchange market. The position is surely this: we have had to borrow abroad quite extensively, wisely or unwisely, in an effort to sustain our standard of living. There are some 7 billion foreign balances in London and it appears that we need to go on borrowing for some time. However, if the willingness to lend dries up or, still more, if the holders of foreign money begin to lose confidence, the fact that, as regards current trade transactions, the pound is undervalued will certainly not avail us.

Clearly, this is what happened, for good reasons or bad. I cannot help thinking that the talk about speculation is very largely beside the point. Perhaps some people have speculated. People usually do; on a small scale. Keynes himself speculated at one time and got very badly burnt. He speculated on the fall of the post-World War I European currencies. However, speculation of that sort is, in my judgment, as dust in the balance; compared to movements which, rightly or wrongly, are actuated by considerations of a commercial or a financial nature. Let us suppose that any of us here was in the unfortunate position of advising an international company with balances in various financial centres or the holder of foreign balances in London. What should we do? Surely, if we were convinced that things here were not wholly satisfactory, we should feel that it was our duty to let our clients know and to tell them that perhaps some other financial centre would be more satisfactory for the time being. Let us suppose that we were importers or exporters; if we were importing and had some fears of a downward movement of sterling, should we not hurry up the payment for our imports before we had to pay more for foreign exchange? If we were exporters, should we not delay bringing home the proceeds for as long as the exchange control would allow us?

My Lords, my purpose in the observations that I am making is simply to explore a little the psychology which I conceive to have been lying behind the adverse movements which caused so much difficulty in the last few weeks. After all, if an adviser loses confidence in the value of a currency, it is his duty to let his employer know. Would noble Lords, if they were in such a position, be prepared to advise their clients to put money into Italy at present? I do not believe that there is anyone who could conscientiously do so. We must recognise the fact that, however wrong-headed we may feel this to be, the foreigner has tended to lose confidence in sterling. Doubtless the arrangements made last weekend will help for the time being. But it is my submission that in the long run confidence in sterling will return only if we ourselves make a conscientious attempt to understand why confidence has tended to ebb. Let me try to facilitate this.

First, despite all that has been done to arrest the rise in costs—and I do not wish to minimise that at all—the prospect for some time ahead is that if nothing further is done we shall still be inflating faster than our competitors; that is to say, the degree of under-valuation will be being whittled away. The prospective rate of inflation for some time is still likely to be too high.

Secondly, there is no guarantee that the planned rate of inflation will not be exceeded. I should hate to be thought to underestimate the great spiritual effort on behalf of the majority of the leaders of the trade unions in agreeing to so marked a change of policy as we have witnessed on their part in the past year. I have no doubt at all that in thus agreeing to recommend restraint they will have brought it about that unemployment will not be so high as might otherwise have been the case.

But the foreign observer, be he right or wrong, will be looking rather at the prospective rate of borrowing and he will see (will he not?) that for a year at least the prospective rate of borrowing is to be higher—unprecedentedly higher—and this in itself will show him, in a simple-minded way, perhaps a glimmer of red light. If he reflects further he may come to the conclusion that, supposing the heralded export-led boom develops—whereas in the past there has been comparative ease in raising government money out of a genuine desire to lend on the part of institutions and private individuals—and the economy starts reviving under the influence of an increased volume of exports (which is not at all improbable), it may be difficult to raise the money by such 'legitimate' means.

I am still trying to depict the frame of mind of the foreign adviser. Thus he may conceive that there may be—to put it mildly—a danger of recourse to increases of financial borrowing, which will not remain idle but which will be spent. If the foreign adviser fears that and if he looks for reassurance at statements made on the part of Her Majesty's Government, particularly statements by the Chancellor of the Exchequer, they will see that there is a certain ambiguity in this respect. There have been no firm pledges that the rate of increase of the various measures of money supply—M1, M3, domestic credit expansion and the like—will fall still further, which is certainly one of the things which are necessary if the planned rate of inflation is not to be exceeded. I ask your Lordships, will the simple-minded foreign adviser, trying to do his duty, be making a complete fool of himself if he argues in this way?

It appears that ministers who travel abroad encounter good friends who do their best to cheer them up, and they have expressed absolutely unlimited confidence in the future of this country—which no doubt is profoundly to be wished for. But having done a little travelling abroad myself, and having talked to a good many foreigners as they pass through London, I must say that my experience has been less reassuring. No single person can possibly assess foreign opinion in the large, but in my experience, at any rate quite a number of foreigners have certain fears for the political unity of this country; and if they take the trouble to peruse the exchanges which take place elsewhere they may not be completely reassured. Here again I am interpreting a point of view of the foreign observers. They will also see a government which commands a minority of votes and which commands an overall majority of one in the other place, pushing ahead with all kinds of things which to them—simple-minded people, who do not understand the frame of mind of this country—may be further inimical to the private sector.

So to cut a long story short, there one has the outlines of a less sanguine view of the future of sterling than has been ventilated from time to time by the supporters of the Government, and which, I suspect, has had much to do with the movements of the exchange rates in recent months. It is clear that the credit arrangements made at the beginning of this week should afford some breathing space. It is obvious in the interests of the great financial centres that they should come together to prevent a collapse in London, if it can be stopped—and the Bank has done nobly. But I emphasise that it is only a breathing space, and if it is not utilised by an attempt to put our house in order it will simply have delayed the moment of truth rather than have averted it.

What, then, should we do? I can understand the unwillingness of the

Government to do something which I certainly have not heard advocated in this debate this afternoon, and that is to resort immediately to panic cuts. Cuts in public expenditure are a very complex business, and if they are not very carefully carried out they cause far more hardship than otherwise need be the case. I personally do not altogether share the optimism concerning the rapidity of the improvement in our position which was ventilated by the noble Lord, Lord Northfield. I am pretty convinced that some cuts will have to come. But, politics apart—which at my age, thank heaven, I have not to worry about—I can see the case for an orderly procedure. No such caution, however, is necessary as regards the future of the credit base. I come back to a point which was made by, I think, the noble Baroness, Lady Seear. What is the argument which would induce the Chancellor of the Exchequer to refrain from giving a more unequivocal guarantee in that respect? Why should he not say that in the next few months the level of M_1, of M_3, of domestic credit expansion or of what-you-will will not be allowed to rise above a certain level?

It is perhaps true, my Lords, that in our slightly insular community, and particularly in Whitehall—I will not say the Treasury, because I never believe in criticising public servants, but in the neighbourhood where ministers responsible for decisions dwell—there is still, I have been told, some scepticism as regards the effectiveness of restraints of this sort. That is doubtless a matter for argument, in good temper, among reasonable men. However, we must recollect that we are unique in entertaining this frame of mind. I think that in all the other leading financial centres of the world quite considerable importance is attached to a due limitation of the money supply in some shape or other. So that if all the others are fools and we alone in the world are right, with our splendid record in the past (if I may so describe it) of controlled inflation, there would still be some advantage in some sort of pledge of this sort. After all, belief in our prospects abroad is not a commodity which we can afford to be without at this moment.

20 The Further Threat to the Pound

Debate on the Address (Second Day); 25 November 1976

My Lords, perhaps I am almost alone in feeling that, with the one notable exception of the speech delivered from these benches by the noble Earl, Lord Cromer, speakers have concentrated perhaps more on long-term problems than on the dangers of the immediate situation. Heaven forbid that I should underestimate the importance of the solution of the long-term problems of this economy! But it is my intense conviction that the solution of these long-term problems will be made much more difficult if we do not succeed in solving the problems which lie nearer at hand.

The present economic situation of this country is truly frightening. Inflation is still proceeding at a rate considerably above that which was promised and, indeed, the rate is threatening to rise once more. Unemployment is high, and there is little prospect of it diminishing rapidly. The credits which earlier in the year were held as saving the situation have proved inadequate. The pound has plunged to levels unprecedented in our history. We have had to apply again for international aid. We have had what I must confess is to me the humiliating spectacle of highly-placed personalities pleading with the financial authorities of other countries who have pursued more prudent policies to increase their risk of increased inflation to help us with our troubles. How has this happened?

As I have just said, the debate this afternoon has concentrated on long-term problems of our inferior productivity. Heaven forbid that I should say or give the impression that I thought that, if our productivity were greater, our position would not be easier! Of course it would be. We had an interesting debate on matters of this kind in the summer, at which many very saddening comparisons were made and some causes indicated. I would not wish to call in question the general attitude which emerged from many of the contributions to that debate, or the additional contributions which have been made this evening. But I must tell your Lordships that, if the current rate of increase of production in this country were doubled or increased beyond that, it would not cure a position in which our aggregate expenditure so greatly exceeds the most optimistic estimates of an immediate increase of production. The simple fact is that, given our contemporary rate of production, our aggregate expenditure has so much

97

exceeded it, and the excess has been so much greater than that of our competitors, that what has happened recently has been inevitable. We have been sustaining our standard of life, in so far as it has been sustained, by borrowing from abroad, and this has become more and more difficult.

But, my Lords, this is an old story. Some of us have been saying something like this for some time. It is even being said now by ministers, as witness the speech of the noble Lord the Lord Privy Seal this afternoon. Indeed some attempts have been made to put it right. Although I confess that my sympathies with some ministers, at any rate, are limited, I would not deny that there has been a considerable change of opinion in the last two years and that there has been a considerable change of policy in certain quarters. Unexpected support has been given to measures which certainly tend in the right direction.

The question is this: why have they been so unsuccessful? Why has the situation deteriorated? It is said with a good deal of plausibility, although I have very great scepticism concerning exact statistical measures in this connection, that at present levels the pound is vastly undervalued. Why is it then that with all the assistance we have received in the past, to which the noble Earl, Lord Cromer, drew attention, the position is so disquieting? Let me say a word first about what I hope your Lordships will agree is a pure fallacy; namely, the suggestion that what has happened recently is all a pure conspiracy, a banker's ramp and so on. I can hardly think of anything sillier in this universe of discourse. If any of us here had money in a foreign centre whose exchange was free and whose policy we distrusted, would not we think of putting some of it in a safer place? Clearly, that is what has been happening to the pound recently. After all, the money which was deposited here, and from whose presence here we have profited in the past, was not ours. It had been lent to us on the assumption that we were safe guardians of its value. Why should we grizzle and grumble if that confidence is now discovered to have been misplaced. There is something frightfully ignominious about the frame of mind from which this sort of explanation springs.

The question, however, remains as to why there should have been this weakening of confidence. If we are honest with ourselves, I suggest the answers are not difficult to seek. I see them, at any rate, in three quarters. First, even if a contemporary comparison of costs should suggest that the pound is undervalued, we should recollect that the inflation here is still continuing, and is still continuing at a rate surpassing that of our competitors. Moreover, even if the incomes policy has been some help hitherto—and I certainly would think it has been successful in avoiding more unemployment than has actually taken place—it is clear that there is going to be much greater difficulty in maintaining it next year. The fact that the unions feel that they have already made tremendous sacrifices, sacrifices which lamentably in the circumstances were insufficient, is certainly going to make the negotiation of an acceptable incomes policy next year harder than in the past. And, at the moment, one of the important factors on the financial side, the money supply, is obviously surpassing the Chancellor's target. It really is not a stupid foreign banker who entertains some hesitation about the future of this country in those circumstances.

Then, secondly—and here I am aware that what I shall say will be very distasteful to some of your Lordships—there is the general direction of domestic policy. I will not dwell on what the noble Lord, Lord Goodman, in this House called the 'Himalayan irrelevance' of the legislation with which our Parliament has been congested recently. I would go further than Lord Goodman; I would say that it was not only irrelevant but in some respects positively detrimental. I do not wish this evening to revive past disputes. I will only say that I do not think that the incentive to leave money here has been increased by what has taken place in the last three months.

Finally, with all respect, I would enumerate the palpable unwillingness in the past of Ministers to face the facts of the situation and to brace themselves to tell the people the full horror of the situation with which we are confronted. How often, my Lords, have I sat through economic debates in this House in which the spokesmen for whatever government were on the front bench; spokesmen for whom I personally had liking, even affection and respect, have made speeches in which, after some allusion to the difficulties of the moment, we have been given to understand that everything now was in splendid hands and further deterioration was unlikely, that a return to growth and prosperity was just round the corner. This was all delivered with such warmth and sincerity that I personally felt something of a cad for some private intellectual reserve in accepting their assurances. As for the pronouncements of those more intimately responsible than anyone in your Lordships' House, I forbear to expatiate. I will only say that since the present Chancellor claimed that he had already reduced inflation to below 10 per cent I feel some mild uneasiness when he deals with figures. I most profoundly hope that he does not say anything of this kind to the highly expert persons with whom he is now negotiating.

Now we have gone to the I.M.F. for a loan. But, again, let us be under no delusion that that means the end of our troubles. As the noble Earl, Lord Cromer, vividly reminded us, out of the loan for which we are asking we are due to repay next month some 1·6 billion dollars advanced us by the central bank loans earlier in the year. I doubt whether our present reserves, without an additional loan, amount to much more than the annual rate of current account deficit registered in the first nine or ten months of this year. Doubtless there are possibilities, and high hopes, obviously, in the bosom of the Prime Minister, of further assistance beyond the I.M.F. money, assuming that to be 'in the bag'. But it should surely be clear to all reflecting persons that the position is not free from further danger, to put it mildly, and we have a long way to go before we are free from the most intense anxiety. But the I.M.F. loan is not yet 'in the bag'. Important talks are still going on.

The noble Lord, Lord Kaldor, rightly reminded us that the I.M.F. was instituted in order to take care of deflationary situations. One of the great troubles of the years since the war is that, preoccupied as we were with the difficulties of the past, we did not foresee that in the future the dangers would be of the reverse order and that inflation rather than deflation would be the order of the day. At any rate, let us not forget that last time we were advised by the International Monetary Fund, at the time of Mr Jenkins' Chancellorship, it was surprising how soon we emerged from our troubles, so that the incoming Conservative Government inherited quite a healthy surplus on balance-of-payments account. I do not think that the situation is so easy this time. What has happened in the last five years has lowered our standing in the world at large, and we have done all sorts of things which have made rehabilitation more difficult.

In considering these matters I think one delusion needs to be overtly dissipated. The current debate is not about deflation. Deflation is a state of affairs in which there is a contraction of spending below the current rate of production at constant prices, as there was a catastrophic deflation in the United States in the 1930s—a catastrophic deflation which some of us, including myself, I am sorry to say, failed to recognise at the time. But we are miles away from that situation today. What we are talking about here, and in the rest of the Western World, is a diminution of the rate of increase in spending which, even in the most prudent economies, certainly exceeds what would have been thought to have been acceptable only ten or twenty years ago.

Finally, whatever our differences of opinion about the minutiae of appropriate policy, the general prescription for countries which are spending more than they earn must be, roughly speaking, the same. If we are lucky—and I pray to heaven that we are—we may get more assistance from abroad to mitigate the ardours and endurances of curbing the fall in the value of our money. But, in the end, the position can only be cured by a narrowing of the gap between spending and production. As I said earlier on, or at any rate hinted, we should be living in a fool's paradise if we think that in the near future production is going to increase so much as to make unnecessary painful adjustments in spending. Equally, anyone who thinks that the wished-for result can be achieved by further 'making the rich squeal', (to use an eloquent expression which I have heard attributed to a highly placed personality), had better have a look at the figures in the invaluable report of the Diamond Commission. The outstanding fact is that for the time being the increase of aggregate spending has to be reduced. While unfortunately all sorts of delusions are still current, I believe that the average man in the street is coming to realise this, and will not complain overmuch of those who have the courage and the candour to tell him the truth about it.

21 Assistance from Abroad and Problems Ahead

Motion: The Economic Situation; 26 January 1977

My Lords, I do not dissent from many speakers in expressing a sense of relief at the present position as compared with the position when we discussed these matters shortly before Christmas. At that time our discussion was under the shadow of a falling pound and uncertainty about the nature of the international assistance which would be forthcoming. Now we have a firm loan from the I.M.F., and arrangements are adumbrated to take care of the sterling balances and, perhaps, to put them on a different footing. The danger at present, so far as I am concerned, is that a state of euphoria should develop in which the continuing difficulties are ignored and the future dangers neglected. I shall not accuse any Member of this House of being in such a state, but one or two remarks which have been made seem to me to err a little towards over-emphasis of the bright side of the picture.

Let me look first at the terms of assistance. I think perhaps I differ slightly from the noble Lord, Lord Thorneycroft, in this respect in that I welcome the assurance that our policy in the next two years will be the subject of a survey by the officials of the International Monetary Fund. If I may say so without offence, I have rather more confidence in their expertise than in that of many former governments of this country. I also welcome the insistence of the International Monetary Fund on explicit conditions, especially the fact that the loan will be doled out at intervals according to our good behaviour. I agree that this is in a sense rather humiliating but nothing—and I repeat, nothing—that has happened in the recent past would have justified any other stipulation on the part of the representatives of the I.M.F.

As to the substantial acceptance of the promised control of public borrowing I confess to thinking that the officials of the I.M.F., who are really not credulous people, have been very good natured. Some of the savings are eyewash. How often, discussing the nationalisation Bills of the last session, did we not hear passionate protestations from the front bench—I remember the noble Lord, Lord Melchett, in particular beating his breast and, not with oaths and curses but with great emphasis, asserting that nationalisation payments were mere transfers. Personally I think things are far more complicated than that. But if you accept that point of view then surely the sale of British Petroleum shares falls into the same category as regards the effect on aggregate expenditure.

For the rest, the savings, although in some cases they are real and important, are obviously the result of political compromise and show a disappointing attempt to get to the real roots of what there is of waste and of expenditure. In this respect I welcome very much the observations which were made by (if I may say so) my noble colleague Lady Seear. I thought she made interesting and useful contributions in that respect; and with others I regard the cuts in defence expenditure rather than more cuts elsewhere as being detrimental to our own national safety and to the stability of the Alliance. But that of course was not the business of the I.M.F.

As to the support of the sterling balance position, I am sure that is in a way reassuring but I do not think we should delude ourselves into thinking that it was prompted by any intense admiration of the record. Sterling is weak on capital account when sterling has been mismanaged, as it has been by successive governments. But the world has something to lose by a collapse and it is that, and not simply our ill-luck (which is sometimes invoked) which has prompted them to make this arrangement. So self-congratulation can surely be a bit overdone. The plain fact is that we have been saved *pro tem.* from a terrible economic disaster by further borrowing from abroad, which eventually will have to be paid back, and by people's unwillingness to see a sudden breakdown of what has hitherto been one of the central elements in international finance. Relief rather than complacency should be the order of the day.

I wish now to look ahead a little at the dangers which are not yet eliminated. It is important that a justifiable sense of the disappearance of certainly immediate dangers, should not dupe us into believing that all our problems are now solved. First, there comes the mere fact of inflation. We are now told that it will continue at its present rate, at least until the summer, which is certainly somewhat different from the claim made some two years ago that it had already been reduced to less than 10 per cent, and, if I may say so, it shows an improvement in candour. We are promised reductions after that. But I wonder whether some of us are not coming to take inflation as a continuing process rather too much for granted. It is perhaps boring to talk about these things, but there are very tangible disadvantages and they deserve to be kept in mind.

Let us first remind ourselves of the arithmetic of the position. Even if we reckon at simple interest, inflation at 10 per cent for ten years would mean that the value of our money would be reduced by half. If it were above that and if we take compound interest into account the prospects are even more terrifying. I know it is unfashionable in certain quarters to express compassion for those who have retired on fixed pension or the accumulation of savings, but your Lordships must know many whose lives have already been darkened in this way by the fall in the purchasing power of the return on investments, which traditional wisdom would have taught them to regard as prudent investments. But let us leave the fixed incomes aside, heavily taxed as some of them are, as the opprobrious recipients of 'unearned' income.

Look at the effect on business. Who can doubt the discouraging effect on investment of the present position? Borrowing at 13 or 14 or more per cent may be all right if inflation is expected to continue. Then you can, of course, pay off what you have borrowed in depreciated money. But supposing inflation is going to come down, as we are promised it will, then the argument cuts the other way. I have no doubt at all that if public borrowing is suitably controlled the recent high rates will come down, but while inflation persists on anything like the scale which enters into conversation about these matters nowadays, unless there is some off-setting policy in the shape of relief of taxation this disincentive will certainly continue.

My Lords, all that would happen if we were the citizens of a closed economy, shut off from the world at large. But living, as we are, in open conditions, as the noble Viscount, Lord Amory, reminded us, inflation at the rate of 15 per cent or 10 per cent is considerably greater than that of our chief competitors. So that if we continue as we are, or even as we are promised to be, it will not be long before the competitive advantage due to undervaluation will tend to vanish. And I must say I do wonder what must be the effect on German or United States representatives—themselves the victims of a rate of diminution of the value of money which a few years ago would have been regarded as causing anxiety—when they are urged by our representatives to increase their inflation in order to get us out of our troubles. I agree with what the noble Lord, Lord Carr, said yesterday; he said that it was unwise to urge this point. I would substitute the word 'naïve' for the word 'unwise'.

So, my Lords, a great responsibility does rest on those who rule over us. Despite my reservations about domestic credit expansion, I think we can rely on the I.M.F. to urge, and perhaps use pressure to see, that financial and fiscal measures are in the right direction. But much, particularly as regards production, depends upon the forthcoming discussions about pay. I confess that I am still sceptical about the idea of a permanent incomes policy. I think that such policies in the past have shown a tendency to break down and to cause all sorts of difficulties. But in present conditions I have no doubt that pay restraint is a matter of the order of the day, and what I fear is that it can easily go wrong. Why do I fear this? I fear it may go wrong in such a way as to upset the recovery which has already been achieved, because in present conditions if the average of basic rates is greatly raised, unemployment, which is deplorable, is likely to go up, and it may well endanger the settlements in which we are rejoicing today. There will be pressure for so-called reflation and that would certainly upset the conditions of the loan.

We must do all we can in other ways to reduce unemployment—retraining, increased mobility, anti-monopoly measures, and so on—but for goodness' sake do not let us increase the rate of increase of inflation.

I think we must face very candidly the fix we are in, and I feel a certain duty to speak in this respect because I must be one of the few people now living who played some part in the devising of the coalition White Paper on *Employment Policy*. Professor Meade is another one still living, and it is to Professor Meade, of course, that what there is of merit in the conception is ultimately due. I can solemnly say that, in the devising of that policy, among officials and among ministers there was certainly no intention to maintain employment resulting from rates of pay greatly in excess of productivity. The intention in that context, with that back history, in which many of us were wrong, the present speaker included, was to avoid unemployment due to positive deflation, such as we had in the 1930s.

It is quite clear that Keynes realised the dangers here, and even Beveridge—in a book about which I have many intellectual reservations—promised 'full employment' at 3 per cent unemployment and emphasised that the success of the policy depended upon wage increases not themselves breeding inflation. But that has been our danger recently. Nothing can be more certain than that if the rate of inflation is being reduced by control of spending excessive increases in pay must cause an increase in a total of unemployment already highly disquieting.

Secondly I suspect that in the next round of discussions on pay restraint the problem of differentials and individual increases will have to be dealt with. So far as the present state of differentials is concerned, there really are very dangerous pressures building up. Quite apart from the absence of training, some, at least, of the shortage of skill, as compared to the super-abundance of less skill, has its origin in the present state of differentials. So far as individuals are concerned, the position is even worse. At the present day the only way open to many high-spirited and efficient young people, anxious to get on in the world and make provision for their wives and families—not such a contemptible motive—the only way to get more than the overall percentage increase in many cases is by changing their jobs. Up to a point this can be overcome—and not dishonestly—by upgrading and reclassification, but only up to a point. The obvious limits are becoming very obvious to many of those whom we most need to keep. I do not think that they will be reassured by what they have heard in this debate. Many of them are asking themselves whether their future and that of their families lies in this country. However, to rectify all that in the context of general pay restraint will require some ingenuity.

Therefore, my Lords, although the problems that lie ahead are not so immediately alarming as they were before Christmas, they are still very formidable.

22 The Threatened Breakdown of Pay Restraint

Motion: The Economic Situation; 20 July 1977

My Lords, the Chancellor's statement last week fell into two parts: the one, the last half, consisted of a number of changes in tax rates and subsidies, the net effect of which he assured us does not seriously affect the general fiscal prospect which he unfolded at the time of the Budget; the other, the first half, outlined a series of alternative prospects of the economy as a whole according to how pay settlements in the future did not or did exceed, on the average, an increase in earnings of 10 per cent. These alternative hypotheses involved a stark and very salutary warning, and it is with that aspect of the statement that I wish to concern myself this afternoon.

I should like to dwell for a moment on recent history. I think there is no question that in the last few months there has been some improvement. Last autumn we were gazing into the abyss as regards the external value of sterling. Up to last week, at any rate, it was stronger. The balance of payments has shown some not inconspicuous improvement. There has been some revival of business confidence.

These relatively cheerful circumstances have a two-fold origin: external aid and greater internal prudence. External aid is obvious, though it is often forgotton. I was relieved when the Lord Privy Seal made a passing allusion to the support that we have received from the authorities of the B.I.S. Where should we be if it had not been for that support and for the I.M.F. loan! Internal prudence has shown itself in the first instance as a curtailment of the prospective rate of increase of aggregate national expenditure. I agree that there has been firmer control of the rate of increase of money supply and some limitation of public borrowing. I hope to high heaven that we can continue to cling to such a policy.

What about pay restraint? Doubtless pay restraint has played some part directly or indirectly in restraining inflation up to date. One has to be a very dyed-in-the-wool monetarist—although I think there is a great deal in the monetarist attitude—to deny all influence on the rate of inflation. But I am sure that the main beneficial effect of pay restraint has been in preventing unemployment from being higher. If rises in earnings had been greater, then unemployment would have been greater too, always assuming that the declared monetary and fiscal policy had continued to hold. But at the same time the policy has been a very blunt instrument. It has upset all sorts of established expectations and relativities. It has upset all sorts of persons; it has created quite glaring anomalies. I have always maintained from the beginning that it would be difficult to sustain it for long, and now this has come true and the outlook is menacing.

I should like to look for a moment at the Chancellor's most optimistic hypothesis: a rate of increase of earnings of not more than 10 per cent. This, he claims, would bring down the rate of inflation to something approaching the rates of our major competitors. I should like to know what figure he has in mind there—the average of the OECD countries? Or perhaps, more tenuous, Germany? I should like to know what assumption he is making concerning the rates of inflation elsewhere. At this stage, in the absence of further information, I will only say this, that given earnings not exceeding 10 per cent it will need a very substantial increase in productivity to bring our inflation down to that of our main competitors. But in any case it is difficult for me to believe that the 10 per cent target will be achieved.

The Chancellor clearly attaches great importance to the 12 months' rule. He asserts that the 12 months' rule should bring it about that many settlements will take place later on, when the rate of inflation may be lower. I doubt very much whether this rule will hold in all its severity. To be restrained into maintaining settlements under Phase 2 until some time in the first half of next year while others are going ahead will certainly impose a degree of self-discipline on those concerned which, frankly, it is not easy to expect with complete confidence.

Quite apart from that, however, the claims which have recently been made by important bodies range much higher than the Chancellor's first hypothesis. As your Lordships will observe, I was not born yesterday, and I have no doubt that some of these claims are preliminary flourishes before getting down to business. But, even so, assuming that those claims, which have been well publicised in the Press, are reduced by half, the inference is still something dangerously more than the 10 per cent hypothesis of the Chancellor.

So supposing the Chancellor's first hypothesis is not realised, what then? The second and third hypotheses both point in the same direction. The rate of inflation will not fall to that of our competitors, and there will be danger of renewed increase of unemployment. Noble Lords should be under no illusion about this. The sort of claims, or even 50 per cent of the claims, already made on behalf of powerful groups are quite incapable of achievement in real terms. The product is not there. The increase of money expenditure will overwhelm it. If the rate of increase of money supply is held constant, therefore, and if such claims are granted, there must be more unemployment.

What then, my Lords, can we do? There are some who argue, with considerable intellectual subtlety, for allowing sterling to appreciate while the going is good. It is true that such appreciation would tend to some reduction in the cost of imports and hence the cost of living. But the extent of the relief which we have to expect in that connection is, to my way of thinking, doubtful. After all, we are still inflating at a rate, roughly speaking, double that of our main competitors. Oil will help so far as the balance of payments is concerned, but the factor of internal cost inflation will work in the other direction. I cannot believe that reliance on possible favourable movements in the rate of exchange, although not to be ruled out in certain circumstances, will see us out of our troubles.

What then? The Trades Union Congress has repudiated an incomes policy, and it is not difficult to understand this attitude, much as one fears, as I fear, its possible consequences. But—I say this with all possible emphasis—the Government cannot afford not to have some sort of incomes policy without abandoning their declared object of economic stabilisation. They cannot afford not to have an incomes policy *at any rate in the sectors of the economy for which they are responsible.* So far as the private sector is concerned, so long as current monetary and fiscal policies persist, there are market influences which should be some safeguard against some inflationary concessions, at least in labour-intensive industries. But where nationalised industries are concerned, like it or not, that is not so. There is an almost ubiquitous assumption that increases there, much larger than is consistent with increases in productivity, can somehow be financed from somewhere. But, my Lords, let there be no mistake: if this assumption is allowed to dominate the situation, and if recourse is had to increased borrowing and the printing press, then the whole future of stabilisation is in jeopardy. That is the chief danger which confronts us in the present situation.

It is not a hopeful picture, and I find it intensely distasteful at this stage in the debate to have to unveil it. But the prospect of an orderly dismantling of the controls of the last two years having collapsed, it is self-deception not to face the picture I have attempted to outline. We shall never get out of our difficulties if we do not foresee them but allow them just to overtake us.

23 The Revival of Sterling and its Problems

Debate on the Address (Second Day); 8 November 1977

My Lords, I want to revert to the themes which were developed by the noble Lord, Lord Peart, in his opening remarks from the Government front bench. I wish that I shared the buoyant confidence which appears to inspire the noble Lord. I personally find the present position an extremely perplexing one. I find it more difficult than almost ever before in my lifetime to peer into the tendencies of the situation in which we find ourselves. I do not know whether to be optimistic or pessimistic. I can see arguments on each side.

First, needless to say, I agree with what the noble Lord said about the comparison between our position today and our position 12 months ago. Surely there can be no question that in several fundamental respects the position has greatly improved. One thinks of the reduction in public sector borrowing requirement. I think that that is a gratifying circumstance. I think that it is a gratifying circumstance that so far the money supply has remained within the limits agreed between the Government and the I.M.F. I find it moderately gratifying that the rate of price increase is now slower, and that the balance of payments is becoming favourable. On all these matters there can surely be no caveat at the claims which the noble Lord made in his opening remarks.

Nor would I wish to dispute his claim that the principles of policy which have been enunciated by various members of the Government in the past few months have been courageous and realistic. I call to mind speeches by the Prime Minister, to the tendency of which, I presume, every right-thinking Member of this House would subscribe. I confess that I found it a little difficult to follow the noble Lord the Lord Privy Seal in his claim that there has been no application of brakes, that there has been complete continuity of policy throughout the tenure of office of the Government which he represents. I found that somewhat of an over-statement. Yet holding the balance as evenly as a cross-bencher can, I must say that I welcomed the admission by the noble Lord, Lord Carr of Hadley, that he would not be willing to claim that his own Governments in the past have been entirely immune from criticism, have been entirely immune from the suspicion, which some of us entertained, that some of the responsibility for the current deplorable state of inflation rests on that side.

Having up to now expressed very substantial agreement with the tone of remarks of the Lord Privy Seal, I must confess that I am unable to share his confident expectation that we are now set fair to recovery. I am unable to share the feeling of general optimism which was diffused throughout the majority of opinion in this country up to a few days ago. Let us suppose that our present policy is successful, and let us suppose that by next spring the rate of inflation is reduced to 10 per cent per annum. I confess that I am surprised that people should view such a state of affairs with any degree of complacency. I find the rate of inflation of 10 per cent per annum a terrifying rate.

I find it a terrifying rate comparatively. It will still be in excess of the rate of inflation of our chief industrial competitors. If it is not reduced still further, then any advantage that we may have reaped by the comparative under-valuation of the pound sterling will very speedily pass away.

But I also find it is a terrifying figure, foreign competition and all that apart, from an absolute point of view. It may very well be that there are some sections of the community which, with the 10 per cent guideline as regards average earnings, can, roughly speaking, keep pace with the deterioration in the purchasing power of money. But there are other members of the community who cannot. It may even be that there are such members of the community in your Lordships' House. I do not think that you can exaggerate the extent to which the current deterioration in the value of money is lowering, not merely the economic well-being of quite important sections of the community, but also the general moral tone of our society, and is spreading cynicism and division among the members of it.

Will this guideline be achieved? I certainly would not stand here and argue that it will not, but I certainly do not think that at this stage we can take it for granted. The 10 per cent guideline was after all, supposed to apply to *earnings*. I have the suspicion that some people think that it applies to basic *rates*, which, of course, as the Chancellor has explained, have to be considerably below 10 per cent if his objective is to be realised; and I thoroughly agree with the noble Baroness, Lady Seear, who reminded us that, in industrial relations, averages tend to be minima. All that may be wrong, but, in any case, at the present time there are some claims outstanding which are wildly in excess of the guideline, and certainly if they were granted, or if you struck an average between the guideline and the claims, we should speedily see the disappearance of our hopes for the slowing down of the inflation, and the strength of the pound would certainly be eroded.

This brings me to the question of the rate of exchange—a hideous question. Here I cannot help thinking that the difficulties of the situation have been to some extent elided in much otherwise well-informed discussion, and, personally, I must confess to real sympathy with the complexities of mind of those having the momentous responsibility of advising the Government in this matter. Needless to say—I hope I need not say it—if the strength of the recent demand for sterling was due solely to the expectation of a solid surplus in the balance of payments, I should decidedly have no objection to a rise in the rate of sterling. Doubtless such a rise would embarrass export industries other than those responsible for the surplus. Nevertheless, I should regard the balance of advantage to the community to be positive from such an appreciation. I certainly do not subscribe to the view that the rate of exchange should be kept low in order to protect export industries, other than oil.

However, the situation is not nearly as simple as that. The recent excess demand for sterling has doubtless been due partly to the prospects of an improving balance of payments, but it is obviously partly speculative, in anticipation of appreciation, and (what is not sufficiently emphasised in the technical discussion) partly due to the prolonged weakness of the dollar. That side of the situation can quite easily turn adverse with very disturbing effects on expectations in our own economy—an adverse turn which would certainly need a strong reserve to cope with it. Certainly, if current fears regarding the tendency of pay claims were to prove well founded, the strength of sterling at the rate prevailing till recently might easily wither away.

In the last analysis I agree with the proposition of the Governor of the Bank of England at the Mansion House banquet. I agree with Mr Richardson's proposition that adherence to monetary targets designed to diminish inflation must be one of the paramount objectives of policy. Let me say at once that this is not—I repeat, not—because I think that the movements of the money supply are the sole cause of inflation. I contend only that adequate limitation of the money supply is essential to cope with other causes.

I admit that, personally, I would have hoped that there were other ways to cope with the excess supplies of foreign currency. I should not have been adverse to more relaxation of the exchange control to offset this inward movement. I do not think such movements as British investment abroad, let alone the use of money to repay the massive debts that we have contracted abroad and which have to be paid off in the first half of the 1980s, would be contrary to the national interest. But, besides that, as the situation built up, I will confess to your Lordships that the thought did cross my mind that some regulations preventing the inflow affecting the money supply, regulations, perhaps, of the kind practised to some extent in Germany and Switzerland, some segregation of deposits of that sort, would not be out of order.

But these are complicated, expert matters. I am prepared to believe that in this respect I may have been wrong in underestimating the difficulties. At any rate, I am wholeheartedly behind the insistence of the Governor of the Bank of England that keeping to the money supply target is very important; so that if, for technical reasons, there was no other way of maintaining this objective, I agree that floating was incumbent. But I do not think we should deceive ourselves in this connection. If the rate of inflation moves up again, a higher rate of exchange will not be with us for long—and that is not a circumstance which causes me any gratification whatever.

Index

Money supply: (*Contd.*)
cent increase, 76; reduction to 16 per cent in 1975 predicted to result in some diminution of economic activity and some diminution of rate of increase of prices, 76; why not announce targets?, 96

Nationalisation: a dubious cure for poor industrial relations, 43
Norms for pay settlements: the dangers of, 33

O'Brien, Lord: tribute to his role in sustaining our international credit, 26; sympathy expressed for his confrontation with public demand for simultaneous support of gilt-edged market and restraint of aggregate expenditure, 40

Pay restraint: main benefit prevention of more unemployment, 86, 105
Phillips Point: 9–10
Price control: undesirable save in cases of long period monopoly, 65; its manifold dangers and administrative difficulties, 68
Productivity in Great Britain: its deficiencies understandable but not main cause of inflation, 1–2, 42–4; per unit of investment poor record as compared with most of our competitors, 9
Projections: are *not* reliable predictions, 9
Public expenditure: rethinking of fundamental principles required, 28

Reflation abroad: understandable reluctance of authorities concerned to increase rates of inflation to bail us out of our self-created difficulties, 103
Regulator, the: insufficient use of regretted, 3
Rent restriction: a definite hindrance to mobility, 16
Richardson, Gordon: his welcome position regarding monetary targets, 110
Rueff, Jacques: his warnings concerning instability of the gold exchange standard, 23

Seear, Lady: the author's concurrence with her view that British inflation not yet hyper-inflation but his insistence that it is nevertheless alarming, 53; agreement with contention that relief of taxation more appropriate for dealing with low-paid than distortions of labour market, 64; her warning that, in industrial relations, averages become minima, 109
Selective employment tax: regretted, 16, 27, 31
Shipping strike of 1966–67: a great embarrassment to policy of the Government, 30
Social contract, alleged: its dubious status, 77
Special Drawing Rights: to be regarded in the late sixties as future safeguard rather than contemporary remedy, 23
Sterling: devaluation November 1967, 18; floating of June 1972, 53; the flight from, summer and autumn 1976, 93–9; eventual foreign support not prompted by admiration of the record, 102; Rate of exchange: undesirability of keeping it artificially low, 110–11

Unemployment: fear of at time of high boom inappropriate, 14; if due to positive deflation, availability of financial remedies, 47; further increase predicted in 1974, 76

Wilberforce Report: probable consequences, 41–4
Wilson, Sir Harold: recall of his assurance that devaluation of 1967 did not imply that money in one's pocket had thereby lost its power to purchase, 31